Betty
KNOX
(incarpotated)

The
Believer's
Prayer Life

(Loneliness)

Politics

difficulties (Bearth)

Conflict (Associate)

Boredom

Anxielty

Depression

(strengthening)
Consideration

The Andrew Murray PRAYER Library

The Believer's Prayer Life

Andrew Murray

BETHANY HOUSE PUBLISHERS

MINNEAPOLIS, MINNESOTA 55438

A Division of Bethany Fellowship, Inc.

Originally entitled, *The Prayer Life*

Copyright © 1983
Bethany House Publishers
All Rights Reserved

Published by Bethany House Publishers
A Division of Bethany Fellowship, Inc.
6820 Auto Club Road, Minneapolis, Minnesota 55438

Printed in the United States of America

Library of Congress Cataloging in Publication Data

Murray, Andrew, 1828-1917.
   The believer's prayer life.

   Translation of: Die gebedslewe.
     1. Prayer. 2. Spiritual life—Reformed authors.
I. Title.
BV210.2.M82713   1983   248.3'2   83-12254
ISBN 0-87123-277-4

The Author

ANDREW MURRAY was born in South Africa in 1828. After receiving his education in Scotland and Holland, he returned to that land and spent many years there as both pastor and missionary. He was a staunch advocate of biblical Christianity. He is best known for his many devotional books.

Other Books by Andrew Murray

Be Perfect
The Believer's Call to Commitment
The Believer's Daily Renewal
The Believer's Secret of Obedience
The Believer's School of Prayer
Day by Day with Andrew Murray
Holy in Christ
How to Raise Your Children for Christ
Jesus Christ: Prophet-Priest
Like Christ
The Master's Indwelling
The Ministry of Intercessory Prayer
Money
New Life
The Secret of Believing Prayer
The Spirit of Christ

Foreword

Knowing the origin of this book, and the object with which it was written, will help the reader better understand its teaching.

It came out of a ministers' conference at Stellenbosch, South Africa, April 11-14, 1912. Professor de Vos, of our Dutch Reformed Theological Seminary, had written a letter to our church ministers concerning the low state of spiritual life which marked the church generally, which ought to lead to the inquiry of how far that statement included our church too. What had been said about the lack of spiritual power in the book, *The State of the Church*, called for deep searching of heart, since he thought the statement was true. He suggested we come together, and in God's presence find the cause of the evil. He wrote: "If we only study the conditions in all sincerity, we shall have to acknowledge that our unbelief and sin are the cause of the lack of spiritual power; that this condition is one of sin and guilt before God, and nothing less than a direct grieving of God's Holy Spirit."

His invitation met with a hearty response. Our four theological professors, with more than two hundred ministers, missionaries, and theological students, met with the above words as the keynote of our meeting. From the very first message, there was a tone of confession as the only way to repentance and restoration. Then opportunity was given for testimony as to what might be the sins which made the life of the church so feeble. Some began to mention failings in conduct, in doctrine or in service, that they had seen in other ministers. Soon it was felt that this was not the right way; each must acknowledge that in which he himself was guilty.

The Lord led us gradually to the sin of prayerlessness as one of the deepest roots of the evil. No one could claim to be free from this. Nothing so reveals a defective spiritual life in minister and congregation as the lack of believing and unceasing prayer. Prayer is the pulse of the spiritual life. It is the great means of bringing to minister and people the blessing and power of heaven. Persevering and believing prayer means a strong and an abundant life.

When the spirit of confession began to prevail, the question arose, would it be possible to gain victory over all that had in the past hindered our prayer life? In smaller conferences held previously, many had been most anxious to make a new beginning, and yet doubted that they would be able to maintain that prayer life which they saw to be in accordance with the Word of God. Often they had made the attempt but had failed. They did not dare to promise the Lord to live and pray as He would have them; they felt it impossible. Such confessions gradually led to the great truth that the only power for a new prayer life is to be found in an entirely new relation to our blessed Savior. As we see in Him the Lord who saves us from sin—the sin of prayerlessness too—our faith yields itself to a life of closer intimacy with Him. Then a life in His love and fellowship will make prayer the natural expression of our soul's life. Before we parted, many testified that they were returning with new light and new hope of finding in Jesus Christ strength for a new prayer life.

Many felt that this was only a beginning. Satan, who had so long prevailed in the place of prayer, would do his utmost again to tempt us to yield to the power of the flesh and the world. Nothing but the teaching and fellowship of Christ himself could give power to remain faithful.

The need was felt for a statement of the truths dealt with at the conference, to remind those who had been present of what they had learned, and of what would help them in the new endeavor after that prayer life which is so essential to a minister's success. It was also needed for those who had been prevented from coming, and for the church elders, who had in many cases felt the deepest interest in hearing of the purpose for which their ministers had attended.

Early copies of the book were sent out with the thought that if the leaders of the church, ministers and elders, begin to see that in spiritual work *everything depends upon prayer,* and that God himself is the helper of those who wait on Him, it would indeed be a day of hope for our church. It was also meant for all believers who long for a life of more complete separation to the Lord. For all who desired to pray more and pray better, it pointed them to the glory of God in our personal place of prayer and the way in which that glory can rest upon the soul.

When first asked to have the book translated into English, I felt that its composition had been too hurried and its tone, because of the close connection with the meetings that had preceded, too colloquial to make this desirable. My own limited strength made it impossible for me to think of rewriting it. When, however, my friend, Rev. W. M. Douglas, asked permission to translate it, I consented. If God has a message through the book to any of His servants, I would count it a privilege to tell what He has done here in our church, as a suggestion of what He may do in other churches.

I close with my greetings to all ministers of the Gospel and church members who may read these pages. The grace

of God manifestly wrought among us conviction of sin, confession of deep need and helplessness, and then gave the
vision and the faith of what Jesus Christ can do for those
who trust Him. I pray fervently that He also may give more
than one who reads courage to take counsel with his brethren, and to seek for and obtain that full fellowship with God
in prayer which is the very essence of the Christian life. It
has been said: "Only the prayerless are too proud to own up
to prayerlessness." Let us believe that many hearts are
waiting for the call inviting them to united and wholehearted confession of shortcoming as the only but the sure way of
a return and restoration to God's favor and the experience
of what He will do in answer to prayer.

I wish to add one word more in regard to "the Pentecos-
tal prayer meetings" held throughout our church. These
have had an interesting and important place in our work.
At the time of the great Revival in America and Ireland in
1858 and following years, some of our elder ministers issued
a circular urging the churches to pray that God might visit
us too. In 1860, revival broke out in various parishes. In
April 1861, there was very deep interest shown in the Paarl
in one of our oldest congregations. During the week preced-
ing Whitsunday the minister, who ordinarily preached only
once on a Sunday, announced that there would be a public
prayer meeting in the church in the afternoon. The occasion
was one of extraordinary interest and many hearts were
deeply touched. As one result the minister suggested that in
the future the ten days between Ascension and Whitsunday
should be observed by daily prayer meetings. This took
place the following year. Such blessing was received that all
the neighboring congregations adopted the ideas, and now
for fifty years these ten days of prayer have been observed
throughout the whole church. Each year notes were issued
as subjects of the messages and prayer. As a result Christians throughout our whole church have been educated in
the knowledge of what God's Word teaches regarding the

Holy Spirit, and have been stirred to seek His blessed leading and yield themselves to it. These ten days have often
led to special effort with the unconverted and partial revival. They have been the means of untold blessing in leading
ministers and people to recognize the place that the Holy
Spirit ought to have as the executive of the Godhead in the
heart of the believers, in the dealing with souls and in
consecration to the service of the Kingdom. Very much is
still lacking of the full knowledge and power of the Holy
Spirit, but we feel that we cannot be sufficiently grateful to
God for what He has done through leading us to dedicate
these days to special prayer for His Holy Spirit to work.

I have written this thinking that some will be glad to
know of it and to unite in the same observance in their
sphere.

Andrew Murray

Contents

PART ONE:

The Prayer Life

1

The Sin of Prayerlessness

If conscience is to do its work and the contrite heart is to feel its misery, it is necessary for each individual to confess his sin by name. The confession must be severely personal. In a meeting of ministers probably no single sin should be acknowledged with deeper shame than the sin of prayerlessness. Each one of us needs to confess, "Guilty."

Why is prayerlessness such a great sin? At first it seems merely a weakness. So much is said about lack of time and all sorts of distractions that the deep guilt of the situation is not recognized. From now on, let it be our honest desire that the sin of prayerlessness may be to us truly sinful.

1. *What a reproach it is to God.* The holy and most glorious God invites us to come to Him, to converse with Him, to ask Him for the things we need, and to experience the depth of blessing there is in fellowship with Him. He has created us in His own image and has redeemed us by His own Son, so that in conversation with Him we might find our highest glory and salvation.

What use do we make of this heavenly privilege? How many there are who take only five minutes for prayer! They say they have no time. The heart desire for prayer is lacking. They do not know how to spend half an hour with God! It is not that they absolutely do not pray; they pray every day—but they have no joy in prayer, as a token of communion with God which shows that God is everything to them.

If a friend comes to visit they have time. They make time—even at the cost of sacrifice—for the sake of enjoying conversation with him. Yes, they have time for everything that really interests them, but no time to practice fellowship with God, and enjoy being with Him! They find time for someone who can be of service to them; but day after day, month after month passes, and there is no time to spend even one hour with God.

Do not our hearts begin to acknowledge that we disrespect and dishonor God to dare to say we cannot find time for fellowship with Him? If this sin begins to appear plain to us, shall we not with deep shame cry out: "Woe is me, for I am undone, O God; be merciful to me, and forgive this awful sin of prayerlessness"?

2. *It is the cause of a deficient spiritual life.* Prayerlessness is proof that, for the most part, our life is still under the power of "the flesh." Prayer is the pulse of life; by it the doctor can diagnose the condition of the heart. The sin of prayerlessness proves to the ordinary Christian or minister that the life of God in the soul is mortally sick and weak.

Much is said and many complaints are made about the feebleness of the Church to fulfill her calling, to exercise an influence over her members, to deliver them from the power of the world, and to bring them to a life of holy consecration to God. Much is also said about her indifference to the millions of heathen whom Christ entrusted to her, to make known to them His love and salvation. What is the reason that many thousands of Christian workers in the world have no greater influence? Nothing except this—the prayerlessness of their service. With all their zeal in study and work in the church, in spite of all their faithfulness in preaching and conversation with the people, they lack that ceaseless prayer which has attached to it the sure promise of the Spirit and power from on high. The sin of prayerlessness is the cause of a powerless spiritual life!

3. *The church suffers dreadful loss as a result of prayer-lessness of the minister.* A minister's business is to train believers for a life of prayer. How can a leader do this if he himself understands little about the art of conversing with God and of receiving from the Holy Spirit each day from heaven abundant grace for himself and for his work? A minister cannot lead a congregation higher than he is himself. He cannot with enthusiasm point out a way or explain a work in which he himself neither walks nor lives.

How many thousands of Christians know next to nothing of the blessedness of prayer fellowship with God! How many know something of it, and long to know more, but in the preaching of the Word they are not persistently urgent to obtain that blessing? The reason is simply and only that the minister understands so little about the secret of powerful prayer, and does not give prayer the place in his service which, in the nature of the case and in the will of God, is indispensably necessary. Oh, what a difference we should notice in our congregations, if ministers could see the sin of prayerlessness in its right light and be delivered from it!

4. *The impossibility of preaching the Gospel to all men*—as we are commanded by Christ to do—as long as this sin is not overcome and cast out.

Many feel that the great need of missions is the obtaining of men and women who will give themselves to the Lord to strive in prayer for the salvation of souls. It has also been said that God is eager and able to deliver and bless the world He has redeemed if His people were only willing and ready to cry to Him day and night. But how can congregations be brought to that without first a complete change in ministers so that they recognize that the indispensable thing is not preaching, not pastoral visitation, not church work, but fellowship with God in prayer until they are clothed with power from on high?

Oh, that all thought and work and expectation concerning the Kingdom might drive us to the acknowledgment of the sin of prayerlessness! God help us to root it out! God deliver us from it through the blood and power of Christ Jesus! God teach every minister of the Word to see what a glorious place he may occupy if he first of all is delivered from this root of evil, so that with courage and joy, in faith and perseverance, he can go on with his God!

The Lord lay the burden of this sin of prayerlessness so heavy on our hearts that we may not rest until it is taken far from us through the name and power of Jesus. He will make this possible for us.

A Witness from America

In 1898, two members of the Presbytery of New York attended the Northfield Conference for the deepening of the spiritual life. They returned to their work with the fire of a new enthusiasm. They endeavored to bring about a revival in the entire Presbytery. In a meeting which they held, the chairman was guided to ask the group about their prayer life. "Brethren," said he, "let us today make confession before God and each other. It will do us good. Will everyone who spends half an hour every day with God in connection with His work, raise your hand?" One hand was held up. He made a further request: "All who spend fifteen minutes in this way, raise your hand." Not half of the hands were held up. Then he said: "Prayer, the working power of the Church of Christ, and half of the workers make hardly any use of it! All who spend five minutes hold up hands." All hands went up. But one man came later with the confession that he was not quite sure if he spent five minutes in prayer every day. "It is," said he, "a terrible revelation of how little time I spend with God."

2

The Cause of Prayerlessness

In an elders' prayer meeting, one brother asked: "What is the cause of so much prayerlessness? Is it unbelief?"

The answer was: "Certainly; but what is the cause of that unbelief?" The disciples asked the Lord Jesus: "Why could not we cast the devil out?" His answer was: "Because of your unbelief." He added: "Howbeit this kind goes not out but by prayer and fasting." If the life is not one of self-denial—of fasting (letting the world go), of prayer (laying hold of heaven), then faith cannot be exercised. In a life lived according to the flesh and not according to the Spirit, we find the origin of the prayerlessness of which we complain. As we left the meeting one brother said to me: "The whole difficulty is that we wish to pray in the Spirit and at the same time walk after the flesh. This is impossible."

If one is sick and desires healing, it is of prime importance that the true cause of the sickness be discovered. This is always the first step toward recovery. If the root problem is not recognized, and attention is directed toward the wrong cause, or to secondary problems, healing is out of the question. In like manner, it is of utmost importance for us to obtain correct insight into the cause of the sad condition of deadness and failure in our private place of prayer, which should be such a blessed place for us. Let us seek to recognize fully the root of this evil.

Scripture teaches us that there are only two conditions possible for the Christian. One is a walk according to the Spirit, the other a walk according the "the flesh." These two powers are in irreconcilable conflict with each other. So most Christians—even though we thank God that they are born again through the Spirit and have received the life of God—still continue to live their ordinary life, not according to the Spirit, but according to "the flesh." Paul writes to the Galatians: "Are you so foolish? having begun in the Spirit, are ye now made perfect by the flesh?" (Gal. 3:3). Their service lay in fleshly outward performances. They did not understand that where "the flesh" is permitted to influence their service of God, it soon results in open sin.

So he mentions as the work of "the flesh" not only grave sins such as adultery, murder, drunkenness, but also the more ordinary sins of daily life—wrath, strife, variance. Then he exhorts: "Walk in the Spirit, and ye shall not fulfil the lust of the flesh. . . . If we live in the Spirit, let us also walk in the Spirit" (Gal. 5:16, 25). The Spirit must be honored not only as the Author of a new life, but also as the Leader and Director of our entire walk. Otherwise we are what the Apostle calls "carnal."

The majority of Christians have little understanding of this matter. They have no real knowledge of the deep sinfulness and godlessness of that carnal nature which belongs to them, and to which unconsciously they yield. "God . . . condemned sin in the flesh" (Rom. 8:3)—in the cross of Christ. "They that are Christ's have crucified the flesh with the affections and lusts" (Gal. 5: 24). "The flesh" cannot be improved or sanctified. "The carnal mind is enmity against God: for it is not subject to the law of God, neither indeed can be" (Rom. 8:7). There is no means of dealing with "the flesh," except as Christ dealt with it, bearing it to the cross. "Our old man is crucified with him" (Rom. 6:6); so we by faith also crucify it, and regard and treat it daily as an accursed thing that finds its rightful place on the accursed cross.

It is sad that so many Christians seldom think or speak earnestly about the deep and immeasurable sinfulness of "the flesh." "In me (that is, in my flesh) dwelleth no good thing" (Rom. 7:18). The man who truly believes this may well cry out: "I see another law in my members. . . . O wretched man that I am! Who shall deliver me from the body of this death?" (Rom. 7:23, 24). Happy is he who can go further and say: "I thank God through Jesus Christ our Lord. . . . For the law of the Spirit of life in Christ Jesus hath made me free from the law of sin and death" (Rom. 7:25; 8:2).

Would that we might understand God's counsels of grace for us! "The flesh" on the cross—the Spirit in the heart and controlling the life.

This spiritual life is too little understood or sought after; yet it is literally what God has promised, and will accomplish in those who unconditionally surrender themselves to Him for this purpose.

Here then we see this deep root of evil as the cause of a prayerless life. "The flesh" can say prayers well enough, calling itself religious for so doing, and thus satisfy conscience. But "the flesh" has no desire or strength for the prayer that strives after intimate knowledge of God, that rejoices in fellowship with Him, and that continues to lay hold of His strength. So, finally, it comes to this—"the flesh" must be denied and crucified.

The Christian who is still carnal has neither disposition nor strength to follow after God. He rests satisfied with the prayer of habit or custom. But the glory, the blessedness of secret prayer, is a hidden thing to him until one day his eyes are opened, and he begins to see that "the flesh," in its disposition to turn away from God, is the archenemy which makes powerful prayer impossible for him.

Once, at a conference, I spoke on the subject of prayer, and used strong expressions about the enmity of "the flesh" as a cause of prayerlessness. After the address, the minister's wife said that she thought I had spoken too strongly. She also had to mourn over too little desire for prayer, but she knew her heart was sincerely set on seeking God. I showed her what the Word of God said about "the flesh," and that everything which prevents the reception of the Spirit is a secret work of "the flesh." Adam was created to have fellowship with God and enjoyed it before his fall. But after the Fall, immediately there came a deep-seated aversion to God, and Adam fled from Him. This incurable aversion is characteristic of the unregenerate nature and the chief cause of our unwillingness to surrender ourselves to fellowship with God in prayer. The following day that woman told me that God had opened her eyes. She confessed that the enmity and unwillingness of "the flesh" was the hidden hindrance in her defective prayer life.

Do not seek to find in circumstances the explanation of this prayerlessness over which we mourn. Seek it where God's Word declares it to be—in the hidden aversion of the heart to a holy God.

When a Christian does not yield completely to the leading of the Spirit—and such a surrender is certainly the will of God and the work of His grace—he lives, without knowing it, under the power of "the flesh." This life of "the flesh" manifests itself in many different ways. It appears:

1. In the hastiness of spirit, or the anger which so unexpectedly arises in you;
2. In the lack of love for which you have so often blamed yourself;
3. In the pleasure found in eating and drinking, about which at times your conscience has chided you;

4. In that seeking for your own will and honor, that confidence in your own wisdom and power, that pleasure in the world, of which you are sometimes ashamed before God.

All this is life "after the flesh." "Ye are yet carnal" (1 Cor. 3:3). Perhaps that text disturbs you at times; you do not have full peace and joy in God.

Take time to answer the question: Have I found here the cause of my prayerlessness, of my powerlessness to effect any change in the matter? I live in the Spirit, I have been born again, but I do not walk after the Spirit—"the flesh" lords it over me. The carnal life cannot possibly pray in the spirit with power. God forgive me. The carnal life is evidently the cause of my sad and shameful prayerlessness.

The Storm Center on the Battlefield

Mention was made in conference of the expression "strategic position" used so often in reference to the great strife between the Kingdom of Heaven and the powers of darkness.

When a general chooses the place from which he intends to strike the enemy, he pays most attention to those points which he thinks most important in the fight. On the battlefield of Waterloo there was a farmhouse which Wellington immediately saw as the key to the situation. He did not spare his troops in his endeavor to hold that point: the victory depended on it. So it actually happened. It is the same in the conflict between the believer and the powers of darkness. The place of private prayer is the key, the strategic position where decisive victory is obtained.

The enemy uses all his power to lead the Christian—and above all the minister—to neglect prayer. He knows that however admirable the sermon may be, however attractive the service, however faithful the pastoral visitation, none of these things can damage him or his kingdom if prayer is neglected. When the Church shuts herself up to the power of the prayer closet, and the soldiers of the Lord have received on their knees "power from on High," then the powers of darkness will be shaken and souls will be delivered. In the church, on the mission field, with the minister and his congregation, everything depends on the faithful exercise of the power of prayer.

In the week of conference I found the following in *The Christian*:

> Two persons quarrel over a certain point. We call them Christian and Apollyon. Apollyon notices that Christian has a certain weapon which would give him a sure victory. They meet in deadly strife, and Apollyon resolves to take away the weapon from his opponent, and destroy it. For the moment the main cause of the strife has become subordinate. Now is the great point: Who shall get possession of the weapon on which everything depends? It is of vital importance to get hold of that.

So it is in the conflict between Satan and the believer. God's child can conquer everything by prayer. Is it any wonder that Satan does his utmost to snatch that weapon from the Christian or to hinder him in the use of it?

How does Satan hinder prayer? By temptation to postpone or curtail it, by bringing in wandering thoughts and all sorts of distractions, through unbelief and hopelessness. Happy is the prayer hero who, through all, takes care to hold fast and use his weapon. Like our Lord in Gethsemane, the more violently the enemy attacked the more earnestly He prayed, and did not stop until He had obtained the victory. After naming all the other parts of the armor, Paul adds: "With all prayer and supplication in the Spirit" (Eph. 6:18). Without prayer, the helmet of salvation, the shield of faith and the Sword of the Spirit, which is God's Word, have no power. All depends on prayer. God teach us to believe and hold this fast!

3

The Fight Against Prayerlessness

As soon as the Christian becomes convinced of his sin in this matter, his first thought is that he must begin to strive, with God's help, to gain the victory over it. But alas, he soon finds that his striving is worth little. The discouraging thought comes over him—he cannot continue faithful! At conferences on the subject of prayer, during the past years, many a minister has said openly that it seemed impossible for him to attain such a strict life.

Recently I received a letter. A minister, well known for his ability and devotion, wrote: "As far as I am concerned, it does not seem to help me to hear too much about the life of prayer, about the strenuous exertion for which we must prepare ourselves, and about all the time and trouble and endless effort it will cost us. These things discourage me—I have heard them so often. Time after time I have put them to the test, and the result has always been sadly disappointing. It does not help me to be told: 'You must pray more, and hold a closer watch over yourself, and become altogether a more earnest Christian.' "

My reply to him was as follows: "I think in all I said at the conference or elsewhere, I have never mentioned exertion or struggle, because I am so entirely convinced that our efforts are futile unless we first learn how to abide in Christ by a simple faith."

My correspondent said further: "The message I need is this: 'See that your relationship to your living Savior is what it ought to be. Live in His presence, rejoice in His love, rest in Him.'" A better message could not be given, if it is only rightly understood. "See that your relationship to the living Savior is what it ought to be." But this is exactly what will make it possible for one to live the life of prayer.

We must not comfort ourselves with the thoughts of standing in a right relationship to the Lord Jesus while the sin of prayerlessness has power over us, and while we, along with the whole Church, have to complain about our feeble life which makes us unfit to pray for ourselves, for the Church, or for missions, as we should. But if we first recognize that a right relationship to the Lord Jesus, above all else, includes prayer, with both the desire and power to pray according to God's will, then we have something which gives us the right to rejoice in Him and to rest in Him.

This incident points out how naturally discouragement will be the result of self-effort, and so block out all hope of improvement or victory. Indeed this is the condition of many Christians when called on to persevere in prayer as intercessors. They feel it is something entirely beyond their reach—they have not the power for the self-sacrifice and consecration necessary for such prayer—they shrink from the effort and struggle which will, as they suppose, make them unhappy. They have tried, in the power of the flesh, to conquer the flesh—a wholly impossible thing. They have endeavored by Beelzebub to cast out Beelzebub—and this can never happen. It is Jesus alone who can subdue the flesh and the devil.

We have spoken of a struggle which will certainly result

in disappointment and discouragement. This is the effort made in our own strength. But there is another struggle which will certainly lead to victory. The Scripture speaks of "the good fight of faith," that is to say, a fight which springs from and is carried on by faith. We must get right conceptions about faith, and stand fast in our faith. Jesus Christ is ever the "Author and Finisher" of faith. When we come into right relationship with Him, we can be sure of the help and power He bestows. Just as earnestly as we must in the first place say: "Do not strive in your own strength. Cast yourself at the feet of the Lord Jesus, and wait upon Him in the sure confidence that He is with you and works in you"; so do we in the second place say: "Strive in prayer; let faith fill your heart—so will you be strong in the Lord, and in the power of His might."

An illustration will help us to understand this. A devoted Christian woman who conducted a large Bible class with zeal and success, once came troubled to her minister. In her earlier years she had enjoyed much blessing in her place of private prayer, in fellowship with the Lord and His Word. But this had gradually been lost, and, do what she would, she could not get right. The Lord had blessed her work, but the joy had gone out of her life. The minister asked what she had done to regain the lost blessedness. "I have done everything," said she, "that I could think of, but all in vain."

He then questioned her about her experience in connection with her conversion. She gave an immediate and clear answer: "At first I spared no pains in my attempt to become better, and to free myself from sin, but it was all useless. At last I began to understand that I must lay aside all my efforts and simply trust the Lord Jesus to bestow on me His life and peace, and He did it."

"Why then," said the minister, "do you not try this again? As you go to pray, however cold and dark your heart may be, do not try in your own might to force yourself into the right attitude. Bow before Him and tell Him that He sees in what a poor state you are and that your only hope is in Him. Trust Him, with a childlike trust, to have mercy upon you, and wait upon Him. With such trust you are in a right relationship to Him. You have nothing—He has everything." Some time later she told the minister that his advice had helped her; she had learned that faith in the love of the Lord Jesus is the only method of getting into fellowship with God in prayer.

Do you not begin to see that there are two kinds of warfare? The first is when we seek to conquer prayerlessness in our own strength. In that case, my advice to you is: "Give up your restlessness and effort; fall helpless at the feet of the Lord Jesus; He will speak the word, and your soul will live." If you have done this, then comes the second message: "This is only the beginning. It will require deep earnestness, the exercise of all your power, and a watchfulness of the entire heart—eager to detect the least backsliding. Above all, it will require the surrender to a life of self-sacrifice that God really desires to see in us and which He will work out for us."

4

How to Be Delivered from Prayerlessness

The greatest stumbling block in the way of victory over prayerlessness is the secret feeling that we shall never obtain the blessing of being delivered from it. Often we have tried, but in vain. Old habits, the power of the flesh, our surroundings with their attractions, have been too strong for us. What good is it to attempt that which our heart assures us is out of our reach? The change needed in the entire life is too great and too difficult. If the question is put: "Is a change possible?" our sighing heart says: "Alas, for me it is entirely impossible!" Do you know why that reply comes? It is simply because you have received the call to prayer as the voice of Moses and as a command of the law. Moses and his law have never yet given anyone the power to obey.

Do you really long for the courage to believe that deliverance from a prayerless life is possible for you and may become a reality? Then you must learn the great lesson that such a deliverance is included in the redemption that is in Christ Jesus, that it is one of the blessings of the New Covenant which God himself will impart to you through Christ

Jesus. As you begin to understand this, you will find that the exhortation, "Pray without ceasing," conveys a new meaning. Hope begins to spring up in your heart, that the Spirit—who has been bestowed on you to cry constantly, "Abba, Father"—will make a true life of prayer possible for you. Then you will hearken, not in the spirit of discouragement, but in the gladness of hope, to the voice that calls you to repentance.

Many a person has turned to his place of prayer, under bitter self-accusation that he has prayed so little, and has resolved for the future to live in a different manner. Yet no blessing has come—there was not the strength to continue faithful, and the call to repentance had no power, because his eyes had not been fixed on the Lord Jesus. If he had only understood, he would have said: "Lord, You see how cold and dark my heart is. I know that I must pray, but I feel I cannot do so. I lack the urgency and desire to pray."

He did not know that at that moment the Lord Jesus in His tender love was looking down upon him and saying: "You cannot pray. You feel that all is cold and dark. Why not give yourself over into My hands? Only believe that I am ready to help you in prayer. I long greatly to pour My love into your heart, so that you, in the consciousness of weakness, may confidently rely on Me to bestow the grace of prayer. Just as I will cleanse you from all other sins, so also will I deliver you from the sin of prayerlessness—only do not seek the victory in your own strength. Bow before Me as one who expects everything from his Savior. Let your soul keep silence before Me, however sad you feel your state to be. Be assured of this—I will teach you how to pray."

Many will acknowledge: "I see my mistake. I had not thought that the Lord Jesus must deliver and cleanse me from this sin also. I had not understood that He was with me every day as I prayed, ready in His great love to keep and bless me, however sinful and guilty I felt myself to be. I had not supposed that just as He will give all other grace in answer to prayer, so, first and most of all, He will bestow the grace of a praying heart. What folly to think that all other blessings must come from Him, but that prayer, on which everything else depends, must be obtained by personal effort! Thank God, I begin to comprehend—the Lord Jesus himself is in my prayer closet watching over me, and holding himself responsible to teach me how to approach the Father. This only He demands—that I, with childlike confidence, wait upon Him and glorify Him.

Have we forgotten this truth? From a defective spiritual life nothing better can be expected than a defective prayer life. It is vain for us, with our defective spiritual life, to endeavor to pray more or better. *It is an impossibility.* It is essential that we experience that he who "is in Christ Jesus is a new creature: old things have passed away; behold, all things are become new." This is literally true for the man who understands and experiences what it is to be in Jesus Christ.

Our whole relationship to the Lord Jesus must be a new thing. I must believe in His infinite love, which longs to have communion with me every moment, and to keep me in the enjoyment of His fellowship. I must believe in His divine power, which has conquered sin and will truly keep me from it. I must believe in Him who, as the great Intercessor, through the Spirit, will inspire each member of His Body with joy and power for communion with God in prayer. My prayer life must be brought entirely under the control of Christ and His love. Then, for the first time, will prayer become what it really is, the natural and joyous breathing of the spiritual life, by which the heavenly atmosphere is inhaled and then exhaled in prayer.

Do you see that when this faith possesses us, the call to a life of prayer which pleases God will be a welcome call? The cry, "Repent of the sin of prayerlessness," will not be responded to by a sigh of helplessness or by the unwillingness of the flesh. The voice of the Father will be heard as He sets

ly opened door and receives us into blessed
himself. Prayer for the help of the Spirit to
er be in fear of an effort too great for our
.. instead, it will be merely falling down in utter weakness at the feet of the Lord Jesus, to find there that victory
comes through the might and love which stream from His
countenance.

Perhaps the question arises in our mind, "Will this continue?" Fear follows, "You know how often you have tried
and been disappointed." But now faith finds strength, not
in the thought of what you will or do, but in the changeless
faithfulness and love of Christ, who once again helps and
assures you that those who wait on Him shall not be
ashamed.

If fear and hesitation still remain, I pray you by the mer-
cies of God in Jesus Christ, and by the unspeakable faithfulness of His tender love, dare to cast yourselves at His
feet. Only believe with your whole heart—there is deliverance from the sin of prayerlessness. "If we confess our sins,
he is faithful and just to forgive us our sins, and to cleanse
us from all unrighteousness" (1 John 1:9). In His blood and
grace there is complete deliverance from all unrighteousness, and from all prayerlessness. Praised be His name for
ever!

5

How Deliverance from Prayerlessness May Continue

What we have said about deliverance from the sin of prayerlessness also applies to answer the question, "How may the experience of deliverance be maintained?" Redemption is not granted to us piecemeal, or as something of which we may use from time to time. It is bestowed as a fullness of grace stored up in the Lord Jesus, which may be enjoyed in new fellowship with Him every day. It is so necessary that this great truth should be driven home and fastened in our minds that I will mention it once more. Nothing can preserve you from carelessness, or make it possible for you to persevere in living, powerful prayer, except daily close fellowship with Jesus our Lord.

He said to His disciples: "Ye believe in God, believe also in me. . . . Believe me that I am in the Father, and the Father in Me. . . . He that believeth on me, the works that I do shall he do also; and greater works than these shall he do" (John 14:1, 11, 12).

The Lord wished to teach His disciples that all they had learned from the Old Testament concerning the power and holiness and love of God must now be transferred to Him. They must not believe merely in certain written documents, but in Him personally. They must believe that He was in the Father, and the Father in Him, in such a sense that they had one life, one glory. All that they knew about Christ, they would find in God. He laid much emphasis on this, because it was only through such a faith in Him and His divine glory that they could do the works which He did, or even greater works. This faith would lead them to know that just as Christ and the Father are one, so also they were in Christ, and Christ was in them.

It is this intimate, spiritual, personal, uninterrupted relationship to the Lord Jesus which manifests itself powerfully in our lives, and especially in our prayer lives. All the glorious attributes of God are in our Lord Jesus Christ. What does this mean?

1. *God's omnipresence*, with which He fills the world, and every moment is present in everything. Like the Father, so now our Lord Jesus is everywhere present, above all with each of His redeemed ones. This is one of the greatest and most important lessons which our faith must learn. We can clearly understand this from the example of our Lord's disciples. What was the peculiar privilege of these disciples, who were always in fellowship with Him? It was uninterrupted enjoyment of the presence of the Lord Jesus. Because of this they were extremely sorrowful at the thought of His death. They would be deprived of that presence. He would be with them no longer. Under these circumstances, how did the Lord Jesus comfort them? He promised that the Holy Spirit from heaven should work in them such a sense of the fullness of His life and of His personal presence that He would be even more intimately near, and have more unbroken fellowship with them, than ever they experienced while He was upon earth.

This great promise is now the inheritance of every believer, although so many of them know little about it. Jesus

Christ, in His divine personality, in that eternal love which led Him to the cross, longs to have fellowship with us every moment of the day, and to keep us in the enjoyment of that fellowship. This ought to be explained to every new convert: "The Lord loves you so, that He would have you near Him without a break that you may have experience of His love." Every believer who has felt his powerlessness for a life of prayer, of obedience, and of holiness must learn this. This alone will give us power as intercessors to conquer the world and to win souls out of it for our Lord.

2. *The omnipotence of God.* How wonderful is God's power! We see it in creation, we see it in the wonders of redemption recorded in the Old Testament. We see it in the wonderful works of Christ which the Father wrought in Him, and above all in His resurrection from the dead. We are called on to believe in the Son, just as we believe in the Father. Yes, the Lord Jesus who, in His love, is so unspeakably near us, is the Almighty One with whom nothing is impossible. Whatever may be in our hearts or flesh which will not submit to us, He can and will conquer. Everything that is promised in God's Word, all that is our inheritance as children of the New Covenant, the almighty Jesus can bestow upon us. If I bow before Him in my prayer closet, then I am in contact with the eternal, unchanging power of God. If I commit myself for the day to the Lord Jesus, then I may rest assured that His eternal, almighty power takes me under its protection, and accomplishes everything for me.

If only we would take time for the hidden place of prayer so that we might experience in full reality the presence of this almighty Jesus! What a blessedness would be ours through faith! An unbroken fellowship with an omnipresent and almighty Lord.

3. *The holy love of God.* This means that He, with His whole heart, offers all His divine attributes for our service, and is prepared to impart himself to us. Christ is the revelation of God's love. He is the Son of that love—the gift of His

love—the power of His love. This Jesus, who tried on the cross to give an overwhelming proof of His love in His death and shedding of His blood—so as to make it impossible for us not to believe in that love—this Jesus is He who comes to meet us in our prayer closet. There He gives positive assurance *that unbroken fellowship with Him is our inheritance. Through Him it will become our experience.* The holy love of God which sacrificed everything to conquer sin and bring it to nothing comes to us in Christ to save us from every sin.

Think over our Lord's words, "Ye believe in God, believe also in me." "Believe me that I am in the Father, and ye in me, and I in you." Those words are the secret of the life of prayer. Take time in your prayer room to bow down and worship. Wait on Him until He unveils himself, takes possession of you, and goes out with you to show how a man may live and walk in abiding fellowship with an unseen Lord.

Do you long to know how you may always experience deliverance from the sin of prayerlessness? Here you have the secret. Believe in the Son of God, give Him time in your inner room to reveal himself in His ever-present nearness, as the Eternal and Almighty One, the Eternal Love who watches over you. Then you will experience something that you possibly have not known before—it has not entered into the heart of man what God can do for those who love Him.

6

The Blessing of Victory

If now we are delivered from the sin of prayerlessness, and understand how this deliverance may continue to be experienced, what will be the fruit of our liberty? He who grasps this truth will seek after this liberty with renewed earnestness and perseverance. His life and experience will indeed be evidence that he has obtained something of unspeakable worth. He will be a living witness of the blessing which victory has brought.

1. *The blessedness of unbroken fellowship with God.* Think of the confidence in the Father which will replace the reproach and self-condemnation which characterized our lives before. Think of the deep consciousness we have that God's almighty grace has effected something in us, proving that we really bear His image and are fitted for a life of communion with Him and prepared to glorify Him. In spite of our conviction of our nothingness, think how we may live as true children of a King, in communion with their Father, and may manifest something of the character of our Lord Jesus in the holy fellowship with His Father which He had when on earth. Think how in our prayer room the hour of prayer may become the happiest time in the whole day for

us, and how God may use us there to share in the carrying out of His plans and make us fountains of blessing for the world around us.

2. *The power which we may have for the work to which we are called.* The preacher will learn to receive his message really from God, through the power of the Holy Spirit, and to deliver it in that power to the congregation. He will know where he can be filled with the love and zeal which will enable him, in his rounds of pastoral visiting, to meet and help each individual in a spirit of tender compassion. He will be able to say with Paul: "I can do all things through Christ who strengtheneth me." "We are more than conquerors through him that loved us." "We were ambassadors for Christ . . . : we pray you in Christ's stead, be ye reconciled to God." These are not vain dreams or pictures of a foolish imagination. God has given us Paul as an illustration, so that, however we may differ from him in gifts or calling, still in inner experience we may know the all-sufficiency of grace which can do all things for us just as it did for him.

3. *The prospect which opens before us for the future*—to be consecrated to take part as intercessors in the great work of bearing on our hearts the need of the entire Church and world. Paul sought to arouse men to pray for all saints, and he tells us what a conflict he had for those who had not yet seen his face. In his personal presence he was subject to conditions of time and place, but in the Spirit he had power in the name of Christ to pray for blessing on those who had not yet heard of the Savior. In addition to his life in connection with men here on earth, far or near, he lived another, a heavenly life—one of love and of a wonderful power in prayer which he continually exercised. We can hardly conceive of the power God will bestow if only we get freed from the sin of prayerlessness, and pray with the daring which reaches heaven and in the almighty name of Christ brings down blessing.

What a prospect! Ministers and missionaries brought by

God's grace to pray, let us say twice as much as formerly, with twofold faith and joy! What a difference it would make in the preaching, in the prayer meeting, in the fellowship with others! What gentle power would come down in a prayer room, sanctified by communion with God and His love in Christ! What influence would be exercised on believers, urging them forward to the work of intercession! How greatly would this influence be felt in the Church and among the heathen! What power might be exercised over ministers of other churches. Who knows how God might use us for His church through the whole world! Is it not worthwhile to sacrifice everything, and to beseech God without ceasing to give us real and full victory over the prayerlessness which has covered us with such shame?

Why do I write these things, and extol so highly the blessedness of victory over "the sin which doth so easily beset us," and which has so terribly robbed us of the power which God has intended for us? I can answer. I know all too well what weak concepts we have concerning the promises and the power of God. I see how prone we always are to backslide, to limit God's power, and to deem it impossible for Him to do greater things than we have seen. It is a glorious thing to get to know God in a new way in our prayer closet. That, however, is but the beginning. It is something still greater and more glorious to know God as the All-Sufficient One, and to wait on His Spirit to open our hearts and minds wide to receive the great things, the new things which He really longs to bestow on those who wait for Him.

God's object is to encourage faith in His children and servants so they understand and rely upon the unspeakable greatness and omnipotence of God, so they take literally, in a childlike spirit, this word: "Now unto him that is able to do exceeding abundantly above all that we ask or think . . . unto him be glory throughout all ages" (Eph. 3:20, 21). Oh, that we knew what a great and glorious God we have!

You ask: "May not this note of certain victory become a snare, and lead to levity and pride?" Undoubtedly. That which is the highest and best on earth is always liable to abuse. How, then, can we be saved from this? Through nothing so surely as through true prayer, which brings us really into contact with God. The holiness of God, sought for in persistent prayer, will cover our sinfulness. The omnipotence and greatness of God will make us feel our nothingness. Fellowship with God in Jesus Christ will lead us to realize that there is in us no good thing, and that we can have fellowship with God only as our faith becomes a humbling of ourselves as Christ humbled himself, and we truly live in Him as He is in the Father.

Prayer is not merely coming to God to ask something from Him. It is above all fellowship with God, and being brought under the power of His holiness and love, till He takes possession of us, and stamps our entire nature with the lowliness of Christ, which is the secret of all true worship.

In Christ Jesus we draw near to the Father just like those who have died with Christ, and have entirely done with their own life, like those in whom He lives and whom He enables to say: "Christ lives in me." What we have said about the work that the Lord Jesus does in us to deliver us from prayerlessness is true not only of the beginning of the life of prayer, and of the joy which a new experience of power to pray causes us, but also for the whole life of prayer all the day long. "Through Him" we have access to the Father. In this, as in the whole spiritual life, "Christ is all." "They saw no man save Jesus only."

May God strengthen us to believe that there is certain victory prepared for us, and that the blessing will be more than the heart of man has conceived! God will do this for those who love Him.

This does not come to us all at once. God has great patience with His children. He bears with us in our slow progress with Fatherly patience. Let each child of God rejoice in all that God's Word promises. The stronger our faith, the more earnestly will we persevere to the end.

7

The More Abundant Life

Our Lord spoke this word concerning the more abundant life when He said that He had come to give His life for His sheep: "I am come that they might have life, and that they might have it more abundantly" (John 10:10). A man may have life, and still through lack of nourishment or through illness, there may be no abundance of life or power. This was the distinction between the Old Testament and the New. In the former there was indeed life, under the Law, but not the abundance of grace of the New Testament. Christ had given life to His disciples, but they could receive the abundant life only through His resurrection and the gift of the Holy Spirit.

All true Christians have received life from Christ. The greater portion of them, however, know nothing about the more abundant life which He is willing to bestow. Paul speaks constantly of this. He says about himself that the grace of God was "exceeding abundant": "I can do all things through Christ who strengtheneth me." "Thanks be unto God, who always causeth us to triumph in Christ." "We are more than conquerors through him that loved us."

45

We have spoken of the sin of prayerlessness, and the means of deliverance, and how to be kept free from it. What has been said on these points is all included in that expression of Christ: "I am come that they might have life, and that they might have it more abundantly." It is of utmost importance for us to understand this more abundant life because, for a true life of prayer it is necessary that we walk in an ever-increasing experience of that overflowing life.

It is possible for us to begin this conflict against prayerlessness in dependence on Christ, looking to Him to be assisted and kept in it, and still be disappointed. This is the time when prayerlessness must be looked upon as the one sin against which we must strive. It must be recognized as part of the whole life of the flesh, and as being closely connected with other sins which spring from the same source. We forget that the entire flesh and all its affections, whether manifested in the body or soul, must be regarded as crucified, and be handed over to death. We must not be satisfied with a feeble life, but must seek for an abundant life. We must surrender ourselves entirely, for the Spirit to take full possession of us, and so manifest that life in us that our spiritual being will be totally transformed. By that the complete control of Christ and the Spirit will be recognized.

What is it, then, which peculiarly constitutes this abundant life? We cannot too often repeat, or in different ways too often set it forth—the abundant life is nothing less than the full Jesus having the full mastery over our entire being, through the power of the Holy Spirit. As the Spirit makes known in us the fullness of Christ and the abundant life which He gives, it will be chiefly in three aspects:

1. *As the Crucified One.* Not merely as the One who died for us, to atone for our sins; but as He who has taken us up with himself on the cross, to die with Him, and who now works out in us the power of His cross and death. You have the true fellowship with Christ when you can say: "I have been crucified with Christ. He, the Crucified One, lives in

me." The feelings, the disposition which was in Him, His lowliness and obedience even to the death on the cross—these were what He referred to when He said of the Holy Spirit: "He shall take of mine, and shall show it unto you"—not as an instruction, but as childlike participation of the same life which was in Him.

Do you desire the Holy Spirit to take full possession of you so as to cause the crucified Christ to dwell in you? This is exactly the purpose for which He has been given, and this He will surely accomplish in all who yield themselves to Him.

2. *As the Risen One.* The Scripture frequently mentions the resurrection in connection with the wonder-working power of God, by which Christ was raised from the dead; and from which comes the assurance of "the exceeding greatness of his power to us-ward who believe, according to the working of his mighty power, which he wrought in Christ, when he raised him from the dead" (Eph. 1:19, 20). Do not pass too quickly from these words. Turn back and read them once more. No matter how powerless and weak you feel, recognize the truth that the omnipotence of God is working in you; and, if you only believe, will give you daily a share in the resurrection of His Son.

Yes, the Holy Spirit can fill you with the joy and victory of the resurrection of Christ, as the power of your daily life, right here in the middle of the trials and temptations of this world. Let the cross humble you to death. God will work out the heavenly life in you through His Spirit. How little we have understood that it is entirely the work of the Holy Spirit to make us partakers of the crucified and risen Christ, and to conform us to His life and death!

3. *As the Glorified One.* The Glorified Christ is He who baptizes with the Holy Spirit. When the Lord Jesus himself was baptized with the Spirit, it was because He had humbled himself and offered himself to take part in John's baptism of repentance—a baptism for sinners—in Jordan.

Even so, when He took upon himself the work of redemption, He received the Holy Spirit to fit Him for His work from that hour until on the cross "He offered himself without spot to God." Do you want this glorified Christ to baptize you with the Holy Spirit? Then offer yourself to Him for His service, to further His great work of making known to sinners the love of the Father.

God help us to understand what a great thing it is to receive the Holy Spirit with power from the glorified Jesus! It means a willingness—a longing of the soul—to work for Him, and, if need be, to suffer for Him. You have known and loved your Lord, you have worked for Him, and have had blessing in that work, but the Lord has more than that to bestow. By the power of the Holy Spirit, He can so work in us, in our brethren around us, and in the ministers of the church as to fill our hearts with adoring wonder.

Have you grasped this truth? The abundant life is neither more nor less than the full life of Christ as the Crucified, the Risen, the Glorified One, who baptizes with the Holy Ghost, and reveals himself in our hearts and lives as Lord of all within us.

Not long ago I read an expression—"Live in what must be." Do not live, limited by your human imagination of what is possible. Live in the Word—in the love, and infinite faithfulness of the Lord Jesus. Even though it goes slowly, with many a stumble, the faith that always thanks Him—not for experiences, but for the promises on which it can rely—goes on from strength to strength, ever increasing in the blessed assurance that God himself will perfect His work in us.

8

The Example of Our Lord

The connection between the prayer life and the Spirit life is close and indissoluble. Not only do we receive the Spirit through prayer, but the Spirit life requires, as an indispensable thing, a continuous prayer life. I can be led continually by the Spirit only as I continually give myself to prayer.

This was very evident in the life of our Lord. A study of His life will give us a wonderful view of the power and holiness of prayer.

Consider His baptism. When He was baptized and prayed, heaven was opened and the Holy Spirit came down upon Him. Christ's surrender of himself to the sinner's baptism in Jordan was also a surrender of himself to the sinner's death. God desired to crown that surrender with the gift of the Spirit for the work that He must accomplish. But this could not have taken place had He not prayed. In the fellowship of worship the Spirit was bestowed on Him to lead Him out into the desert to spend forty days there in prayer and fasting. Mark 1:32-35 says: "And at even, when the sun did set, they brought unto him all that were diseased, and them that were possessed with devils. And all the city was gathered together at the door. . . . And in the morning, rising up a great while before day, he went out, and departed into a solitary place, and there prayed."

The work of the day and evening had exhausted Him. In His healing of the sick and casting out devils, power had gone out of Him. While others still slept, He went away to pray and to renew His strength in communion with His Father. He had need of this, otherwise He would not have been ready for the new day. The holy work of delivering souls demands constant renewal through fellowship with God.

Think again of the calling of the Apostles as given in Luke 6:12, 13: "And it came to pass in those days, that he went out into a mountain to pray, and continued all night in prayer to God. And when it was day, he called unto him his disciples: and of them he chose twelve, whom also he named apostles." Is it not clear that if anyone wishes to do God's work, he must take time for fellowship with Him, to receive His wisdom and power? The dependence and helplessness of which this is evidence open the way and give God the opportunity of revealing His power. How great was the importance of the choosing of the Apostles for Christ's own work, for the early church, and for all time! It had God's blessing and seal; the stamp of prayer was on it.

Read Luke 9:18, 20: "And it came to pass, as he was alone praying, his disciples were with him: and he asked them, saying, Whom say the people that I am? . . . Peter answering said, The Christ of God." The Lord had prayed that the Father might reveal to them who He was. It was in answer to that prayer that Peter said: "The Christ of God"; and the Lord then said: "Flesh and blood hath not revealed it unto thee, but my Father which is in heaven" (Matt. 16:17). This great confession was the fruit of prayer.

Read on in Luke 9:28-36: "He took Peter and John and James, and went up into a mountain to pray. And as he prayed, the fashion of his countenance was altered, . . . and there came a voice out of the cloud, saying, This is my beloved Son: hear him." Christ had desired that, for the strengthening of their faith, God might give them an assurance from heaven that He was the Son of God. Prayer obtained for our Lord Jesus himself, as well as for His disciples, what happened on the Mount of Transfiguration.

Does it not become still more clear that what God wills to accomplish on earth needs prayer as its indispensable condition? There is but one way for Christ and believers. A heart and mouth open toward heaven in believing prayer will certainly not be put to shame.

Read Luke 11:1-13: "As he was praying in a certain place, when he ceased, one of his disciples said unto him, Lord, teach us to pray." And then He gave them that inexhaustible prayer: "Our Father which art in heaven." In this He showed what was going on in His heart when He prayed that God's name might be hallowed, His kingdom come, His will be done, and all of this "on earth as it is in heaven." How will this ever come to pass? Through prayer. This prayer has been uttered through the ages by countless millions, to their unspeakable comfort. But do not forget this—it was born out of the prayer of our Lord Jesus. He had been praying and therefore was able to give that glorious answer.

John 14:16 says, "I will pray the Father, and he shall give you another Comforter." The entire dispensation of the New Testament, with the wonderful outpouring of the Holy Spirit, is the outcome of the prayer of the Lord Jesus. It is as though God had impressed on the gift of the Holy Spirit this seal—in answer to the prayer of the Lord Jesus, and later of His disciples, the Holy Spirit will surely come. But it will be in answer to prayer like that of our Lord, in which He took time to be alone with God and in that prayer offered himself wholly to God.

Read John 17, the high-priestly, most holy prayer! Here the Son prays first for himself, that the Father will glorify

Him by giving Him power for the cross, by raising Him
from the dead, by setting Him at His right hand. These
great things could not take place save through prayer.
Prayer had power to obtain them.

Afterwards He prayed for His disciples that the Father
might preserve them from the evil one, might keep them
from the world, and might sanctify them. Further on, He
prayed for all those who through their Word might believe
on Him, that all might be one in love even as the Father and
the Son were one. This prayer gives us a glimpse into the
wonderful relationship between the Father and the Son. It
teaches us that all the blessings of heaven come, and continue to come, through the prayer of Him who is at God's
right hand and ever prays for us. But it teaches us, also,
that all these blessings must in the same manner be desired
and asked for by us. The whole nature and glory of God's
blessings consist in this—they must be obtained in answer
to prayer, by hearts entirely surrendered to Him, and
hearts that believe in the power of prayer.

Now we come to the most remarkable instance of all. In
Gethsemane we see that our Lord, according to His constant habit, consulted and arranged with the Father the
work He had to do on earth. First He besought Him in
agony and bloody sweat to let the cup pass from Him. When
He understood that this could not be, then He prayed for
strength to drink it, and surrendered himself with the
words: "Thy will be done." He was able to meet the enemy
full of courage, and in the power of God gave himself over to
the death on the cross. *He had prayed.*

Why have God's children so little faith in the glory of
prayer as the great power for subjecting our own wills to
that of God, as well as for the confident carrying out of the
work of God in spite of our great weakness? Learn from our
Lord Jesus how impossible it is to walk with God, obtain
God's blessing or leading, or do His work joyously and fruit-
fully, apart from close, unbroken fellowship with Him who

is ever a living fountain of spiritual life and power.

Think over this simple study of the prayer life of our Lord Jesus. Then, with prayer for the leading of the Holy Spirit, endeavor to learn from God's Word what the life is which the Lord Jesus Christ bestows upon every Christian and supports in him. It is nothing other than a life of daily prayer. Let each minister especially recognize how entirely useless it is to attempt to do the work of our Lord in any other way than that in which He did it. Let us, as workers, believe that we are set free from the ordinary business of the world, that we may, above everything, have time, in our Savior's name, and with His Spirit, and in oneness with Him, to ask for and obtain blessing for the world.

9

The Holy Spirit and Prayer

Is it not sad that our thoughts about the Holy Spirit are so often coupled with grief and self-reproach? Yet He bears the name of Comforter, and is given to lead us to find in Christ our highest delight and joy. Sadder still is this: He who dwells within us to comfort us is often grieved by us, because we will not permit Him to accomplish His work of love. What a cause of inexpressible pain to the Holy Spirit is all this prayerlessness in the Church! It causes the low vitality and utter impotence so often found in us, because we do not permit the Holy Spirit to lead us.

God grant that our meditation on the work of the Holy Spirit may cause rejoicing and the strengthening of our faith!

The Holy Spirit is "the Spirit of Prayer." He is definitely called by this name in Zech. 12:10: "The spirit of grace and of supplications." Twice in Paul's Epistles there is a remarkable reference to Him in the matter of prayer. "Ye have received the Spirit of adoption, whereby we cry, Abba, Father" (Rom. 8:15). "God hath sent forth the Spirit of his Son into your hearts, crying, Abba, Father" (Gal 4:6). Have you ever meditated on these words: "Abba, Father"?

54

In that name our Savior offered His greatest prayer to the Father, accompanied by the total surrender and sacrifice of His life and love. The Holy Spirit is given for the express purpose of teaching us, right from the very beginning of our Christian life, to utter that word in childlike trust and surrender. In one of these passages we read, "We cry"; in the other, "He cries." What a wonderful blending of the Divine and human cooperation in prayer. What a proof that God has done His utmost to make prayer as natural and effectual as the cry of a child to an earthly father, as he says, "Abba, Father."

Is it not proof that the Holy Spirit is often a stranger in the Church when prayer, for which God has made such provision, is regarded as a task and a burden? Does not this teach us to seek for the deep root of prayerlessness in our ignorance of, and disobedience to, the Divine Instructor whom the Father has commissioned to teach us to pray?

If we wish to understand this truth still more clearly, see Rom. 8:26, 27: "Likewise the Spirit also helpeth our infirmities: for we know not what we should pray for as we ought: but the Spirit itself maketh intercession for us with groanings which cannot be uttered. And he that searcheth the hearts knoweth what is the mind of the Spirit, because he maketh intercession for the saints according to the will of God." Is it not clear? The Christian if left to himself does not know how to pray nor how he ought to pray. But God has stooped to meet us in this helplessness of ours by giving us the Holy Spirit himself to pray for us. That operation of His Spirit is deeper than our thought or feeling, but is acknowledged and answered by God.

Our first work, therefore, ought to be to come into God's presence not with our ignorant prayers, not with many words and thoughts, but in the confidence that the Divine work of the Holy Spirit is being carried on within us. This confidence will encourage reverence and quietness, and will also enable us, in dependence on the help which the Spirit gives, to lay our desires and heart-needs before God. The

supreme lesson for every prayer is—first of all to commit
yourself to the leading of the Holy Spirit and, in total dependence on Him, give Him first place. Through Him your
prayer will have a value you cannot imagine. Through Him
also you will learn to express your desires in the name of
Christ.

What a protection this faith would be against deadness
and despondency in our place of prayer! Only think of it! In
every prayer the Triune God takes a part—the Father who
hears, the Son in whose name we pray, the Spirit who prays
for us and in us. How important it is that we should be in
right relationship to the Holy Spirit and understand His
work!

The following points demand serious consideration.

1. *Let us firmly believe as divine reality that the Spirit
of God's Son, the Holy Spirit, is in us.* Do not assume that
you know this and have no need to reconsider it. It is a
thought so great and divine that it can gain entrance to our
hearts, and be retained there only by the Holy Spirit himself. "The Spirit beareth witness with our spirit." Our position ought to be that of reckoning with full assurance of
faith that our heart is His temple, that He dwells within us
and rules soul and body. Let us thank God heartily when-
ever we pray, that we have His Spirit in us to teach us to
pray. Thanksgiving will draw our hearts toward God and
keep us engaged with Him; it will take our attention from
ourselves, and give the Spirit room in our hearts.

No wonder we have been prayerless, and have felt this
work too heavy for us, if we have tried to have fellowship
with the eternal God apart from His Spirit, who reveals the
Father and the Son.

2. *As we put this faith into practice in the certainty that
the Spirit dwells and works in us, there must also be an understanding of all that He desires to accomplish in us.* His
work in prayer is closely connected with His other work. In
an earlier chapter we saw that His first and greatest work is
to reveal Christ in His omnipresent love and power. So in

prayer the Holy Spirit will constantly remind us of Christ, of His blood and name, as the sure ground of our being-heard.

Then as the Spirit of Holiness He will teach us to recognize and hate and be finished with sin. He is the Spirit of Light and Wisdom, who leads us into the heavenly secret of God's overflowing grace. He is the Spirit of Love and Power, who teaches us to witness for Christ, and to labor for souls with tender pity. The more closely I associate all these blessings with the Spirit, the more shall I be convinced of His Deity, and shall be all the more ready to commit myself to His guidance, as I give myself to prayer. What a different life mine would be if I knew the Spirit as the Spirit of Prayer! Still another thing which I need constantly to learn again is that:

3. *The Spirit desires full possession of my life.* We pray for more of the Spirit, and we pray well if alongside this prayer we set the truth that the Spirit wants more of me. The Spirit would possess me entirely. Just as my soul has my whole body for its dwelling place and service, so the Holy Spirit would have my body and soul as His dwelling place, entirely under His control. No one can continue long and earnestly in prayer without beginning to perceive that the Spirit is gently leading to an entirely new consecration, of which previously he knew nothing. "I seek Thee with my whole heart." The Spirit will make such words more and more the motto of our lives. He will cause us to recognize that what remains in us of doublemindedness is truly sinful. He will reveal Christ as the Almighty Deliverer from all sin, who is always near to defend us. He will lead us in this way in prayer. He will help us to forget ourselves. He will make us willing to offer ourselves for training as intercessors, to whom God can entrust the carrying out of His plans, and who day and night cry to Him to avenge His church of her adversary.

God help us to know the Spirit and to reverence Him as the Spirit of Prayer!

10

Sin

To understand grace, to understand Christ aright, we must understand what sin is. How can we come to this understanding? Only through the light of God and His Word.

Come with me to the beginning of the Bible. See there man created by God, after His image, and pronounced by his Creator to be very good. Then sin entered, as rebellion against God. Adam was driven out of Paradise, and was brought along with the untold millions of following generations under curse and ruin. That was the work of sin. Here we learn its nature and power.

Come further on and see the Ark of Noah on Ararat. So terrible had godlessness become among men that God saw nothing possible except to destroy man from the earth. That was the work of sin.

Come with me to Sinai. God wished to establish His covenant with a new nation—with the people of Israel. But because of man's sinfulness, He could do this only by appearing in darkness and lightning so terrible that Moses said: "I exceedingly fear and quake." And before the end of the giving of the law, that awful message came: "Cursed is every one that continueth not in all things that are written

58

in the book of the law to do them." It was sin which made that necessary.

Come once more with me, this time to Calvary. There see what sin is, and shown in the hatred and enmity with which the world cast out and crucified the Son of God. There sin reached its climax. There Christ was made sin and became a curse by God himself as the only way to destroy sin. In Gethsemane's agony when He prayed that He might not drink the terrible cup, and in the agony on the cross with its deep darkness of desertion, when He cried out: "My God, my God, why hast thou forsaken me?"*we obtain a faint idea of the curse and indescribable suffering which sin brings. If anything can make us hate and detest sin, it is Christ on the cross.

Next come to see the judgment seat of the Great Day, and the bottomless pit of darkness wherein countless souls will be plunged under the sentence: "Depart from me ye cursed, into everlasting fire." When these words truly penetrate our hearts, do they fill us with a never-to-be-forgotten horror of sin, so that we may hate it with a perfect hatred?

What else can help us to understand what sin is? Turn your eyes inward to behold your own heart and see the sin there. All that you have already seen of the hatefulness and godlessness of sin should teach you what sin in your own heart signifies and reveals—all the enmity against God, all the ruin of men, all of its inner nature of hatefulness. These all lie hidden in the sin you have committed and which still dwells in your heart. Remember that you are a child of God. Still, sometimes you commit sin. You allow it to fulfill its lust. Are you not forced to cry out with shame: "Woe is me, because of my sin"? "Depart from me, for I am a sinful man, O Lord."

One great power of sin is that it blinds men so that they do not recognize its true character. Even the Christian himself finds an excuse in the thought that he can never be perfect, and that daily sin is a necessity. He is so accustomed to the thought of sinning that he has almost lost the power and ability to mourn over sin. But there can be no real progress in grace apart from an increased consciousness of the sin and guilt of every transgression against God. And there cannot be a more important question than this: "How can I regain the lost tenderness of conscience, and become prepared really to offer to God the sacrifice of a broken heart?"

Scripture teaches us the way. Remember what God thinks about sin—the hatred with which His holiness burns against it, the solemn sacrifice which He made to conquer sin, and deliver us from it. Tarry in God's presence until His holiness shines upon you, and you cry out with Isaiah: "Woe is me, for I am undone!"

Remember the cross and what the love of Christ had to endure there in the unspeakable pain which sin caused Him. Ask if this will teach us to listen to the voice which says: "Do not this abominable thing which I hate." Take time, so that the blood and love of the cross may exercise their full influence. Think of sin as nothing less than giving one's hand to Satan and his power. Is not this the terrible result of our prayerlessness and of our short and hasty waiting before God—that the true knowledge of sin is almost lost?

Think not only of what redemption has cost Christ, but also of the fact that Christ is offered, by the Holy Spirit, as a gift of inconceivable grace, through whom divine forgiveness and purification and renewing have come. Ask how such love should be repaid. If only time were taken to linger in God's presence and ask such questions, the Spirit of God would accomplish His work of conviction of sin in us. He would teach us to take an entirely new standpoint, and would give us a new view of sin. The thought would begin to arise in our hearts that we have truly been redeemed, so that in Christ's power we may live every day as partners in the great victory which He obtained over sin on the cross, and manifest it in our walk.

What do you think? Do you begin to see that the sin of prayerlessness has had a more terrible effect than you supposed at first? Because of this hasty and superficial communion with God, the sense of sin is so weak that no motives have power to help you to hate sin and flee from it as you ought. Nothing, except the hidden, humble, constant fellowship with God can teach you, as His child, to hate sin as God wants you to hate it. Nothing but the constant nearness and unceasing power of the living Christ can make it possible for you rightly to understand what sin is, and to detest it. Without this deeper understanding of sin, there will be no thought of appropriating the victory which Christ Jesus made possible for you and which would be worked out in you by the Spirit.

O my God, cause me to know my sin, and teach me to tarry before You and to wait on You until Your Spirit causes something of Your holiness to rest upon me! Help me to recognize my sin. Let this drive me to listen to the promise: "He that abideth in him sinneth not." Help me to expect the fulfillment from You!

11

The Holiness of God

It has often been said that the conception of sin and of
the holiness of God has been lost in the Church. In the secret place of prayer we may learn again how to give God's
holiness the position it should have in our faith and life. If
you do not know how to spend half an hour in prayer, take
up the subject of God's holiness. Bow before Him. Give
yourself time, and also give God time, that He and you may
come into touch with one another. It is an effort, but one
fraught with great blessing.

To strengthen yourself in the practice of this Holy Presence, take up the Holy Word. Take the book of Leviticus,
and notice how God five times gives the command: "Ye
shall be holy, for I am holy" (11:44, 45; 19:2; 20:7, 26). Still
more frequent is the expression: "I am the Lord that doth
sanctify you." This great thought is carried over into the
New Testament. Peter says (1 Pet. 1:15, 16): "Be ye holy
in all manner of conversation; because it is written, Be
ye holy; for I am holy." Paul writes in his first Epistle
(1 Thess. 3:13; 4:7; 5:24): "[That] he may stablish your
hearts unblameable in holiness. . . . God hath . . . called us

unto holiness. . . . Faithful is he that calleth you, who also will do it."

Nothing but the knowledge of God as the Holy One will make us holy. How are we to obtain that knowledge of God unless we go alone to Him in our place of prayer? It is a thing utterly impossible unless we take time and allow the holiness of God to shine on us. How can any man on earth obtain intimate knowledge of another man of remarkable wisdom, if he does not associate with that man and remain under his influence? And how can God himself sanctify us if we do not take time to be brought under the power of the glory of His holiness? Nowhere can we get to know the holiness of God, and come under its influence and power, except in our prayer closet. It has been well said: "No man can expect to make progress in holiness who is not often and long alone with God."

And what now is this holiness of God? It is the highest and most glorious and most all-embracing of all the attributes of God. Holiness is the most profound word in the Bible. It is a word that is at home in heaven. Both the Old and New Testaments tell us this. Isaiah heard the seraphs with veiled faces cry out: "Holy, holy, holy, is the Lord of hosts" (6:3). John heard the four living creatures say: "Holy, holy, holy, Lord God Almighty" (Rev. 4:8). This is the highest expression of God's glory in heaven, by beings who live in His immediate presence and bow low before Him. Do we dare imagine that we—by thinking, and reading, and hearing—can understand or become partakers of the holiness of God? What folly! May we begin to thank God that we have our private prayer room, a place where we can be alone with Him. There, may we pray, "Let Your holiness, O Lord, shine more and more into our hearts that they may become holy."

And let our hearts be deeply ashamed of our prayerlessness, through which we have made it impossible for God to impart His holiness to us. Let us ask God fervently to forgive us this sin, and to draw us to Him by His heavenly grace, and to strengthen us to have fellowship with Him, the holy God.

The meaning of the words, "The holiness of God," is not easily expressed. But we may begin by saying that they imply the unspeakable aversion and hatred with which God regards sin. If you wish to understand what that means, remember that He preferred to see His Son die rather than that sin should reign. Think of the Son of God, who gave up His life rather than act in the smallest matter against the will of the Father. He had such a hatred of sin that He preferred to die rather than that men should be held in its power. That is something of the holiness of God, which is a pledge that He will do everything for us—for you and me—to deliver us from sin. Holiness is the fire of God that will consume sin in us and make us holy sacrifices, pure and acceptable before Him. For this reason the Spirit came down as fire. He is the Spirit of God's holiness, the Spirit of sanctification in us.

Think about the holiness of God, then bow in lowliness before Him until your heart is filled with the assurance of what the Holy One will do for you. Take a week, if necessary, to read and reread the words of God on this great truth until your heart is brought under the conviction: "This is the glory of the secret place of prayer, to be able to converse with God the Holy One; to bow in deep humility and shame before Him, because we have so despised Him and His love through our prayerlessness." There we shall receive the assurance that He will again take us into fellowship with himself. No one can expect to understand and receive the holiness of God who is not often and long alone with God.

Someone has said that the holiness of God is the expression of the unspeakable distance by which He in His righteousness is separated from us, and yet also of the unspeakable nearness in which He in His love longs to hold fellowship with us and dwell in us. Bow in humble reverence as you think of the immeasurable distance between you and God. Bow in childlike confidence in the unspeakable desire of His love to be united with you in the deepest intimacy; and reckon most confidently on Him to reveal something of His holiness to the soul which thirsts after Him and waits upon Him and is quiet before Him.

Notice how the two sides of the holiness of God are united in the cross. So terrible was the aversion and anger of God against our sin that Christ was left in the thick darkness, because God had to hide His face from Christ when sin was laid upon Him. Still, so deep was the love of God toward us, and He so desired to be united to us, that He spared not His Son but gave Him over to unutterable sufferings so that He might receive us in union with Christ into His holiness, and embrace us as His beloved children. It was of this suffering that our Lord Jesus said: "I sanctify myself, that they also might be sanctified through the truth" (John 17:19). Thus He is become of God our sanctification, and we are holy in Him.

I beg you not to think lightly of that grace—that you have a holy God who longs to make you holy. Obey the voice of God which calls you to give time to Him in the stillness of your prayer closet so that He may cause His holiness to rest on you. Let it be your business every day, in the secrecy of that prayer room, to meet the holy God. You will be repaid for the trouble it may cost you. The reward will be sure and rich. You will learn to hate sin, and to regard it as accursed and conquered. The new nature will give you a horror of sin. The living Jesus, the holy God, will, as Conqueror, be your power and strength; and you will begin to believe the great promise contained in 1 Thess. 5:23, 24: "The very God of peace sanctify you wholly; . . . Faithful is he that calleth you, who also will do it."

12

Obedience

In opposition to sin stands obedience. "For as by one man's disobedience many were made sinners, so by the obedience of one shall many be made righteous. . . . Ye became the servants of righteousness" (Rom. 5:19; 6:18). In connection with all that has been said about sin, and the new life, and the reception of the Holy Spirit, we must always give to obedience the place assigned to it by God.

It was because Christ humbled himself and became obedient unto death, yea, the death on the cross, that God so highly exalted Him. In this connection Paul exhorts us: "Let this mind be in you, which was also in Christ Jesus" (Phil. 2:5). We see, above everything else, that the obedience of Christ, so pleasing to God, must become the basic characteristic of our disposition and of our entire walk. Just as a servant knows that he must first obey his master in all things, so the surrender to an implicit and unquestioning obedience must become the essential characteristic of our lives.

How little this is understood by Christians! How many allow themselves to be misled, and rest satisfied with the thought that sin is a necessity, that one must sin every day! It would be difficult to say how great is the harm which has been done by this mistake. It is one of the chief causes why the sin of disobedience is so little recognized. I have myself heard Christians, speaking about the cause of darkness and weakness, say, half-laughingly: "Yes, it is just disobedience again." As speedily as possible we try to get rid of a servant who is habitually disobedient. But that a child of God should be disobedient every day is not regarded as anything extraordinary. Disobedience is daily acknowledged, but even so there is no turning away from it.

Is this the reason why so much prayer for the power of the Holy Spirit is offered, and yet so few answers come? Do we not read that "God has given His Holy Spirit to them that obey Him"? Every child of God has received the Holy Spirit. If he uses the measure of the Holy Spirit which he has, with the definite purpose of being obedient to the utmost, then God can and will favor him with further manifestations of the Spirit's power. But if he permits disobedience to get the upper hand, day by day, he need not be surprised if his prayer for more of the Spirit remains unanswered.

We have already said that we must not forget that the Spirit desires to possess more of us. How can we fully surrender ourselves to Him other than by being obedient? The Scripture says that we must be led by the Spirit, that we must walk by the Spirit. My right relationship to the Holy Spirit is that I allow myself to be guided and ruled by Him. Obedience is the most important factor in our whole relationship to God. "Obey My voice, and I will be your God."

Notice how the Lord Jesus, on the last night when giving His great promise about the Holy Spirit, emphasized this point. "If ye love me, keep my commandments. And I will pray the Father, and he shall give you another Comforter" (John 14:15, 16). Obedience was essential as preparation for the reception of the Spirit. This thought is often repeated by Him. "He that hath my commandments, and keepeth them, he it is that loveth me: and he that loveth me shall be loved of my Father, and I will love him, and will manifest

68

myself to him" (John 14:21). So also in verse 23: "If a man love me, he will keep my words: and my Father will love him, and we will come unto him, and make our abode with him." "If ye abide in me, and my words abide in you, ye shall ask what ye will, and it shall be done unto you" (15:7). "If ye keep my commandments, ye shall abide in my love" (v. 10). "Ye are my friends, if ye do whatsoever I command you" (v. 14).

Can words more plainly or forcefully declare that the whole life, in this new dispensation since the resurrection of Christ, depends on obedience? That was the attitude of Christ's life. He lived to do not His own will, but the will of the Father. And He cannot with His Spirit make an abiding home in the heart of one who does not surrender himself utterly to a life of obedience.

It is sad how few are truly concerned about this disobedience! How little we believe the fact that Christ really asks for, and expects this from us—because He has undertaken to make it possible for us. How much is it manifested in prayer, or our walk, or in the depths of our spiritual life, that we really try to please the Lord in all things? Too seldom we mention our disobedience or say, "I will be sorry for my sin."

But is obedience really possible? It certainly is for the man who believes that Christ Jesus is his sanctification and relies on Him.

It is impossible for a man whose eyes have not yet been opened, to see that Christ can at once forgive his sin. Such a man also finds it impossible to see that there is in Christ a sure promise of power to accomplish all that God desires from His child. Just as we found the fullness of forgiveness through faith, so through a new act of faith, a real deliverance from the dominion of sin which so easily ensnares us is obtained. So the abiding blessing of this continuous experience of Christ's keeping power becomes ours. This faith obtains a new insight into promises whose meaning was not previously understood: "The God of peace . . . make you perfect in every good work to do his will, working in you that which is wellpleasing in his sight, through Jesus Christ" (Heb. 13:20, 21). "Unto him that is able to keep you from falling . . . be glory and majesty" (Jude 24, 25). "Give diligence to make your calling and election sure: for if ye do these things, ye shall never fall" (2 Pet. 1:10). "To the end he may stablish your hearts unblameable in holiness" (1 Thess. 3:13). "But the Lord is faithful, who shall stablish you, and keep you from evil" (2 Thess. 3:3).

The fulfillment of these and other promises is secured for us in Christ. Just as certainly as the forgiveness of sin is assured to us in Him, so also is power against new or fresh attacks of sin assured to us. Then for the first time we understand that faith can confidently rely upon a full Christ and His abiding protection.

This faith sheds a totally new light on the life of obedience. *Christ holds himself responsible to work this out in me every moment if I only trust Him for it.* Then I begin to understand the important phrase with which Paul begins and closes Romans: "The obedience of faith" (Rom 1:5; 16:26). Faith brings me to the Lord Jesus, not only for forgiveness of sin, but also every moment to enjoy the power that enables me, as a child of God, to abide in Him, and to be numbered among His obedient children. It is written of these children that, as He who has called them is holy, so they also may be holy in all their behavior. Everything depends on whether or not I believe on the whole Christ, with the fullness of His grace, and that He will be—not now and then but every moment—the strength of my life. Such faith will lead to an obedience which will enable me to "walk worthy of the Lord unto all pleasing, being fruitful in every good work, strengthened with all might, according to his glorious power."

The soul which feeds on such promises will experience, instead of the disobedience of self-effort, all that the obedience of faith means. All such promises have their measure, their certainty, and their strength in the living Christ.

13

The Victorious Life

We viewed the chapter on "The More Abundant Life" mainly from the side of our Lord Jesus. We saw that there is to be found in him—the Crucified, the Risen, the Glorified One who baptized with the Holy Spirit—all that is needed for a life of abundant grace. Now, in speaking of "The Victorious Life," we shall look from another standpoint. We want to see how a Christian can live really as a victor. Often we have repeated that the prayer life is not something which can be improved by itself. So intimately is it bound up with the entire spiritual life that only when that whole life (previously marked by lack of prayer) becomes renewed and sanctified can prayer have its rightful place of power. We must not be satisfied with less than the victorious life to which God calls His children.

Our Lord, in the seven letters to the churches in Revelation, concludes with a promise to those who overcome. Go over that seven-times-repeated phrase, "Him that overcometh," and notice what unspeakable and glorious promises are there given. They were given even to churches like Ephesus that had lost its first love, to Sardis which "had a name to live but was dead," and Laodicea, with her lukewarmness and self-satisfaction—as proof that, if only they would repent, they might win the crown of victory. The call comes to every Christian to strive for the crown. If everything is not sacrificed to gain the victory, how is it possible to be a healthy Christian or to preach in the power of God? It is not; it is impossible.

Then how do we attain victory? The answer is simple. All is in Christ. "Thanks be unto God, which always causeth us to triumph in Christ" (2 Cor. 2:14). "In all these things we are more than conquerors through him that loved us" (Rom. 8:37). It all depends on our right relationship to Christ, our complete surrender, perfect faith, and unbroken fellowship with Him. But how do you attain all this? These simple directions show the way by which the full enjoyment of what is prepared for you in Christ may be yours. They are:

1. A new discovery of sin
2. A new surrender to Christ
3. A new faith in the power which will make it possible for you to persevere

1. *A new discovery of sin.* In Romans 3, you find described the knowledge of sin which is necessary in repentance, for forgiveness—"that every mouth may be stopped, and all the world may become guilty before God" (v. 19). There you took your stand, you recognized your sin more or less consciously, and confessed it, and you obtained mercy. But if you would lead the victorious life, something more is needed. This begins with the recognition that in you, that is, in your flesh, there dwells no good thing (Rom. 7:18). In the inner man you delight in the law of God, but you see another law in your members bringing you into captivity to the law of sin, and compelling you to cry out: "O wretched man that I am! who shall deliver me from the body of this death?" (vv. 23, 24). This is not like your experience at conversion, when you thought over your few or many sins. This work goes much deeper. You find that, as a Christian, you

have no power to do the good that you wish to do. You must be brought to a new and deeper insight into the sin of your nature, and, even though you are a Christian, you must see your utter weakness to live as you ought. You will learn to cry out: "I am a wretched man, a prisoner bound under the law of sin! Who shall deliver me?"

The answer to this question is: "I thank God, through Jesus Christ our Lord" (v. 25). Then follows the revelation of what there is in Christ. It is not limited to what is given in Romans 3. It is more. "I am in Christ Jesus, and the law of the Spirit of life in Christ Jesus hath made me free from the law of sin and death," under which I was bound. I have been made free by the law (or power) of the life of the Spirit in Christ, and now am called, in a new sense and by a new surrender, to acknowledge Christ as the bestower of the victory.

2. *A new surrender to Christ.* You may have used these words "surrender" and "consecration" many times, but without a right understanding of what they mean. As you have been brought by the teaching of Romans 7 to a complete sense of the hopelessness of leading a true Christian life, or a true prayer life, by your own efforts, you begin to realize that the Lord Jesus must take you up by His own power in an entirely new way, and must take possession of you by His Spirit to an entirely new degree. This alone can preserve you from constantly sinning afresh. This only can make you really victorious. This leads you to look away from yourself, to get truly free from yourself, and to expect everything from the Lord Jesus.

If we begin to understand this, we are prepared to admit that in our nature there is nothing good, that it is under a curse, and is nailed with Christ to His cross. We come to see what Paul means when he says that we are dead to sin by the death of Christ. Thus do we obtain a share of the glorious resurrection life there is in Him. With this insight we are encouraged to believe that Christ, through His life in us, through His continual indwelling, can keep us. Just as we had no rest till we knew He had received us at our conversion, so now we feel the need of coming to Him, to receive from Him the assurance that He has really undertaken to keep us by the power of His resurrection life. And we feel then that there must be an act as definite as His reception of us at conversion, by which He gives us the assurance of victory. And although it appears to us to be too great and too much, still the man who casts himself, without plea, into the arms of Christ will experience that He does indeed receive us into such a fellowship as will make us, right from the beginning, "more than conquerors."

3. *A new faith in the power which will make it possible for you to persevere.* You have heard of Keswick,* and the truth for which it stands. It is that Christ is prepared to take upon himself the care and preservation of our lives every day, and all the day long, if we trust Him to do it. In the testimony given by many, this thought is emphasized. They have told us that they felt themselves called to a new surrender, to a complete consecration of life to Christ, but they were hindered by the fear of failure. The thirst after holiness, after an unbroken fellowship with Jesus, after a life of persevering childlike obedience, drew them one way. But the question arose: "Shall I continue faithful?" And to this question there came no answer until they believed that the surrender must be made, not in their own strength, but in a power which was bestowed by a glorified Lord. He would not only keep them for the future, but He must first make possible for them the surrender of faith which expects that future grace. It was in the power of Christ himself that they were able to present themselves to Him.

Oh, Christian, only believe it, there is a victorious life. Christ, the Victor, is your Lord, who will undertake for you in everything, and will enable you to do all that the Father expects from you. Be of good courage. Will you not trust

---

* The Keswick Convention, born out of the Moody-Sankey revival of 1875, highlights topics of prayer, Bible study, and foreign missions. The aim of this annual convention is to promote "practical holiness."

Him to do this great work for you who has given His life for you, and has forgiven your sins? Only dare, in His power, to surrender yourself to the life of those who are kept from sin by the power of God. Along with the deepest conviction that there is no good in you, confess that you see in the Lord Jesus all the goodness of which you have need, for the life of a child of God. Begin literally to live "by the faith of the Son of God, who loved you, and gave himself for you."

For your encouragement, let me give the testimony of Bishop Moule, a man of deep humility and tender piety. When he first heard of Keswick he was afraid of "perfectionism," and would have nothing to do with it. Unexpectedly, during a vacation in Scotland, he came in contact with some friends at a small convention. There he heard an address by which he was convinced how entirely the teaching was according to Scripture. There was no word about sinlessness in the flesh or in man. It was a setting forth of how Jesus can keep a man with a sinful nature from sin. The light shone into his heart. He who had always been counted a sensitive, obedient Christian came in touch now with a new experience of what Christ is willing to do for one who gives himself completely to Him.

Listen to what Bishop Moule says about the text: "I can do all things through Christ who strengtheneth me."

I dare to say that it is possible for those who really are willing to reckon on the power of the Lord, for keeping and victory, to lead a life in which His promises are taken as they stand, and are found to be true. It is possible to cast all our care on Him daily, and to enjoy deep peace in doing it. It is possible to have the thoughts and imaginations of our hearts purified in the deepest meaning of the word, through faith. It is possible to see the will of God in everything, and to receive it, not with sighing, but with singing. It is possible, in the inner life of desire and feeling, to lay aside all bitterness, and wrath, and anger, and evil speaking, every day and every hour. It is possible, by taking complete refuge in divine power, to become strong through and through; and where previously our greatest weakness lay, to find that the things which formerly upset all our resolves to be patient, or pure, or humble, furnish today an opportunity to make sin powerless—through Him who loved us, and works in us an agreement with His will, and a blessed sense of His presence and His power. These things are divine possibilities, and because they are His work, the true experience of them will always cause us to bow lower at His feet, and to learn to thirst and long for more. We cannot possibly be satisfied with anything less than to walk with God—each day, each hour, each moment, in Christ, through the power of the Holy Spirit.

Thank God, a life of victory is sure for those who have a knowledge of their inward ruin and are hopeless in themselves, but who, in "the confidence of despair," have looked to Jesus. They, in faith in His power to make the act of surrender possible for them, have done it in His might, and now rely on Him alone every day and every hour.

PART TWO:

The Inner Room

1

Suggestions for Private Prayer

At the conference, a brother who had earnestly confessed his neglect of prayer, but who was able, later, to declare that his eyes had been opened to see the Lord really supplies grace for all that He requires of us, asked if some suggestions could not be given as to the best way of spending time profitably in our private prayer room. There was no opportunity then for giving an answer. Perhaps the following thoughts may help:

1. As you enter your prayer closet, let your first work be to thank God for the unspeakable love which invites you to come to Him, and to converse freely with Him. If your heart is cold and dead, remember that religion is not a matter of feeling, but first involves the will. Raise your heart to God and thank Him for the assurance you have that He looks down on you and will bless you. Through such an act of faith you honor God, and draw your soul away from being occupied with itself. Think also of the glorious grace of the Lord Jesus, who is willing to teach you to pray, and to give you the disposition to do so. Think, too, of the Holy Spirit who was purposely given to cry "Abba, Father" in your

79

heart, and to help your weakness in prayer. Five minutes spent in this way will strengthen your faith. Once more I say—begin with an act of thanksgiving, and praise God for your place of prayer and the promise of blessing there.

2. You must prepare yourself for prayer by prayerful Bible study. The great reason why the quiet time is not attractive is that people do not know how to pray. Their stock of words is soon exhausted, and they do not know what further to say, because they forget that prayer is not a soliloquy, where everything comes from one side; but it is a dialogue, where God's child listens to what the Father says, and replies to it, and then asks for the things he needs.

Read a few verses from the Bible. Do not concern yourself with the difficulties contained in them. You can consider these later; but take what you understand, apply it to yourself, and ask the Father to make His Word light and power in your heart. Thus you will have material enough for prayer from the Word which the Father speaks to you; you will also have the liberty to ask for things you need. Keep on in this way, and the prayer closet will become at length, not a place where you sigh and struggle only, but one of living fellowship with the Father in heaven. Prayerful study of the Bible is indispensable for powerful prayer.

3. When you have thus received the Word into your heart, turn to prayer. But do not attempt it hastily or thoughtlessly, as though you knew well enough how to pray. Prayer in our own strength brings no blessing. Take time to present yourself reverently and in quietness before God. Remember His greatness and holiness and love. Think over what you wish to ask of Him. Do not be satisfied with going over the same things every day. No child goes on saying the same thing day after day to his earthly father.

What you talk about with the Father is colored by the needs of the day. Let your prayer be something definite, arising either out of the Word which you have read, or out of the real spiritual needs which you long to have satisfied.

Let your prayer be so definite that you can say as you go out, "I know what I have asked of my Father, and I expect an answer." It is a good plan sometimes to take a piece of paper and write down what you wish to pray for.

4. What has been said is in reference to your own needs. But you know that we are allowed to pray that we may help also with the needs of others. One great reason why daily prayer does not bring more joy and blessing is that it is too selfish. Selfishness is the death of prayer.

Remember your family; your congregation, with its interests; your own neighborhood; and the church to which you belong. Let your heart be enlarged, and take up the interests of missions and of the church throughout the whole world. Become an intercessor, and you will experience for the first time the blessedness of prayer as you find out that God will make use of you to share His blessing with others through prayer. You will begin to feel that there is something worth living for, as you see that you have something to say to God. You will find that He from heaven will do things in answer to your prayers which otherwise would not have been done.

A child can ask his father for bread. A full-grown son converses with him about all the interests of his business and about his further purposes. A weak child of God prays only for himself; a full-grown man in Christ understands how to consult with God over what must take place in the Kingdom. Let your prayer list bear the names of those for whom you pray—your minister, and all other other ministers, and the different missionary affairs with which you are connected. Thus the inner room will really become a wonder of God's goodness and a fountain of great joy. It will become the most blessed place on earth. It seems hard to believe, but it is the simple truth, that God will make it a Bethel, where His angels shall ascend and descend, and where you will cry out: "The Lord shall be my God." He will make it also a Peniel, where you will see the face of

God, as a Prince of God, as one who wrestled with the angel and overcame him.

5. Do not forget the close bond between the inner room and the outside world. The attitude of the inner prayer room must remain with us all the day. The object of the secret prayer room is so to unite us to God that we may have Him always abiding with us. Sin, thoughtlessness, yielding to the flesh, or the world, unfit us for prayer and bring a cloud over the soul. If you have stumbled or fallen, return to your secret place, let your first work be to invoke the blood of Jesus and to claim cleansing by it. Rest not till you have fully confessed, repented of, and put away your sin. Let the precious blood of Jesus really give you a fresh freedom of approach to God. Remember that the roots of your life in the inner room reach far out in body and soul, so as to manifest themselves in business life. Let "the obedience of faith," in which you pray in secret, rule you constantly. The inner room is intended to bind man to God, to supply him with power from God, to enable him to live for God alone. God be thanked for that place, and for the blessed life which He will enable us there to experience and nourish.

2

Time

Before the creation of the world time did not exist. God lived in eternity in a way which we little understand. With creation, time began, and everything was placed under its power. God has placed all living creatures under a law of slow growth. Think of the length of time it takes for a child to become a man in body and mind. In learning, in wisdom, in business, in handicraft, and in politics, everything somehow depends on patience and perseverance. Everything needs time.

It is just the same in religion. There can be no converse with a holy God, no fellowship between heaven and earth, no power for the salvation of the souls of others, unless much time is set apart for it. Just as it is necessary for a child to eat and learn every day for many years, so the life of grace entirely depends on the time men are willing to give to it day by day.

The minister is appointed by God to teach and help those who are engaged in ordinary occupations of life to find time and use it correctly for the preservation of the spiritual life. The minister cannot do this unless he himself has a living experience of a life of prayer. His highest calling is not preaching, or speaking, or church visitation, but it is to cultivate the life of God daily, and to be a witness of what the Lord teaches him and accomplishes in him.

Was it not so with the Lord Jesus? Why must He, who had no sin to confess, sometimes spend all night in prayer to God? Because the divine life had to be strengthened in an intimate relationship with His Father. His experience of a life in which He took time for fellowship with God has enabled Him to share that life with us.

Oh, that each minister might understand that he has received his time from God to wait on Him! God must have for fellowship with himself the first and the best of your time. Without this, your preaching and labor have little power. Here on earth I may expend my time in exchange for money or learning. The minister can exchange his time for divine power and the spiritual blessings to be obtained from heaven. That, and nothing else, makes him a man of God, and ensures that his preaching will be in the demonstration of the Spirit and power.

3

The Example of Paul

*"Be ye followers of me, even as I also am of
Christ" (1 Cor. 11:1).*

1. *Paul was a minister who prayed much for his congregation.* Let us read his words prayerfully and calmly so that
we may hear the voice of the Spirit.

"Night and day praying exceedingly that we . . . might
perfect that which is lacking in your faith. . . . The Lord
make you to increase . . . to the end he may stablish your
hearts unblameable in holiness" (1 Thess. 3:10-13).

"The very God of peace sanctify you wholly . . ."
(1 Thess. 5:23).

What food for meditation!

"Now our Lord Jesus Christ himself . . . comfort your
hearts, and stablish you in every good word and work"
(2 Thess. 2:16, 17).

*"Without ceasing I make mention of you always in my
prayers;* making request . . . that I may impart unto you
some spiritual gift, to the end ye may be established"
(Rom. 1:9-11).

"My heart's desire and prayer to God for Israel is, that they might be saved" (Rom. 10:1).

"I . . . *cease not . . . making mention of you in my prayers*; that the God of our Lord Jesus Christ . . . may give unto you the spirit of wisdom and revelation in the knowledge of him . . . that ye may know . . . what is the exceeding greatness of his power to us-ward who believe" (Eph. 1:15-19).

"*For this cause I bow my knees unto the Father* . . . that he would grant you . . . to be strengthened with might by his Spirit in the inner man; that Christ may dwell in your hearts by faith; that ye, being rooted . . . in love . . . might be filled with all the fulness of God" (Eph. 3:14-19).

"*Always in every prayer of mine for you all making request* with joy . . . I pray that your love may abound yet more and more . . . that ye may be sincere . . . filled with the fruits of righteousness" (Phil. 1:4-11).

"But my God shall supply all your need according to his riches in glory by Christ Jesus" (Phil. 4:19).

"*We . . . do not cease to pray for you*, and to desire that ye might be filled with the knowledge of his will . . . that ye might walk worthy of the Lord . . . strengthened with all might, according to his glorious power. . ." (Col. 1:9-11). "I would that ye knew *what great conflict I have for you* . . . as many as have not seen my face in the flesh; that their hearts might be comforted, being knit together in love. . ." (Col. 2:1, 2).

What a study for the prayer closet, to teach us that unceasing prayer formed a large part of Paul's service in the Gospel. We see the high spiritual aim which he set before himself, in his work on behalf of believers, and the tender and self-sacrificing love with which he ever continued to think of the Church and its needs. Let us ask God to bring each one of us and all the ministers of His Word to a life of which such prayer is the healthy and natural outflow. We shall need to turn again and again to these pages if we would really be brought by the Spirit to the apostolic life which God has given us as an example.

2. *Paul was a minister who asked his congregation to pray much.* Read again with prayerful attention:

"I beseech you, brethren, for the Lord Jesus Christ's sake, and for the love of the Spirit, *that ye strive together with me in your prayers to God for me*; that I may be delivered from them that do not believe in Judaea. . ." (Rom. 15:30, 31).

"We . . . trust . . . in God . . . that he will yet deliver us; *ye also helping together by prayer for us*. . ." (2 Cor. 1:9-11).

"*Praying always with all prayer and supplication* in the Spirit, and watching thereunto with all perseverance and supplication for all saints; *and for me*, that utterance may be given unto me, that I may open my mouth boldly, to make known the mystery of the Gospel . . . as I ought to speak" (Eph. 6:18-20).

"For I know that this shall turn to my salvation *through your prayer*, and the supply of the Spirit of Jesus Christ" (Phil. 1:19).

"*Continue in prayer*, and watch in the same with thanksgiving; *withal praying also for us*, that God would open unto us a door of utterance, to speak . . . as I ought to speak" (Col. 4:2-4).

"Finally, brethren, *pray for us*, that the Word of the Lord may have free course, and be glorified, even as it is with you" (2 Thess. 3:1).

What a deep insight Paul had as to the unity of the Body of Christ, and the relation of the members one to another! As we permit the Holy Spirit to work powerfully in us, He will reveal this truth to us, and we too shall have this insight. What a glimpse he gives us of the power of the spiritual life among these Christians, by the way in which he reckoned that at Rome, and Corinth, and Ephesus, and Colosse, and Philippi, there were men and women on whom he could rely for prayer that would reach heaven, and had power with God! What a lesson for all ministers, to lead them to inquire if they truly appreciate the unity of the Body at its right value; ask if they are endeavoring to train up Christians as intercessors. Ask if they indeed understand that Paul had that confidence because he himself was so strong in prayer for the congregation. Let us learn the lesson, and beseech God that ministers and congregations together may grow in the grace of prayer, so that all their service and Christian life may witness that the Spirit of prayer rules them. Then we may be confident that God will avenge His own elect which cry out day and night unto Him.

4

Ministers of the Spirit

What is the meaning of the expression: "The minister of the Gospel is a minister of the Spirit" (2 Cor. 3:6-8)? It means:

1. The preacher is entirely under the power and control of the Spirit, so that he may be led and used by the Spirit as He wills.

2. Many pray for the Spirit, that they may make use of Him and His power for their work. This is certainly wrong. It is He who must use you. Your relationship towards Him must be one of deep dependence and utter submission. The Spirit must have you completely, and always, and in all things under His power.

3. There are many who think they must only preach the Word, and that the Spirit will make the Word fruitful. They do not understand that it is the Spirit, in and through the preacher, who will bring the Word to the heart. I must not be satisfied with praying to God to bless, through the operation of His Spirit, the word that I preach. The Lord wants me to be filled with the Spirit: then I shall speak as I should aright, and my preaching will be in the manifestation of the Spirit and power.

4. We see this on the day of Pentecost. They were filled with the Spirit and began to speak, and spoke with power through the Spirit who was in them.

5. Thus we learn what the relationship of the minister towards the Spirit should be. He must have a strong belief that the Spirit is in him, that the Spirit will teach him in his daily life, and will strengthen him to bear witness to the Lord Jesus in his preaching and visiting. He must live in ceaseless prayer that he may be kept and strengthened by the power of the Spirit.

6. When the Lord promised the Apostles that they should receive power, when the Holy Spirit had come upon them, and commanded them to wait for Him, it was as though He had said: "Do not dare to preach without this power. It is the indispensable preparation for your work. Everything depends on it."

7. What then is the lesson we may learn from the phrase "ministers of the Spirit"? How little we have understood this! How little we have lived in it! How little we have experienced the power of the Holy Spirit! What must we do then? There must be deep confession of guilt that we have so constantly grieved the Spirit, because we have not lived daily as His ministers. There must be simple, childlike surrender to His leading, in sure confidence that the Lord will work a change in us. Then there must be daily fellowship with the Lord Jesus in ceaseless prayer. He will bestow on us the Holy Spirit, like rivers of living waters.

5

The Word and Prayer

Little of the Word, with little prayer, is death to the spiritual life. Much of the Word, with little prayer, gives a sickly life. Much prayer with little of the Word gives more life, but without steadfastness. A full measure of the Word and prayer each day gives a healthy and powerful life. Think of the Lord Jesus. In His youth and manhood, He treasured the Word in His heart. He showed that the Word of God filled His heart—in the temptation in the wilderness, and on every opportunity that presented itself—until He cried out on the cross in death: "My God, my God, why hast thou forsaken me?"

In His prayer life He manifested two things. First, He showed that the Word supplies us with material for prayer, and encourages us in expecting everything from God. The second is that it is only by prayer that we can live such a life that every word of God can be fulfilled in us. And how then can we come to this, so that the Word and prayer may each have its undivided right over us? There is only one answer. Our lives must be wholly transformed. We must get a new, a healthy, a heavenly life, in which the hunger after God's Word and the thirst after God express themselves in prayer

as naturally as do the needs of our earthly life. Every manifestation of the power of the flesh in us, and the weakness
of our spiritual life, must drive us to the conviction that
God, through the powerful operation of His Holy Spirit, will
work out a new and strong life in us.

Oh, that we but understand that the Holy Spirit is es-
sentially the Spirit of the Word and the Spirit of Prayer. He
will cause the Word to become a joy and a light in our souls.
He will also most surely help us in prayer to know the mind
and will of God, and find in it our delight. If we as ministers
wish to explain these things, and to train God's people for
the inheritance which is prepared for them, then we must
commit ourselves from this moment forward to the leading
of the Holy Spirit. We must, by faith in what He will do in
us, appropriate the heavenly life of Christ as He lived it
here on earth, with certain expectation that the Spirit, who
filled Him with the Word and prayer, will also accomplish
that work in us.

Let us believe that the Spirit who is in us is the Spirit of
the Lord Jesus, and that He is in us to make us truly partakers of His life. If we firmly believe this, and set our
hearts upon it, then there will come a change in our involve-
ment with the Word and prayer such as we could not have
thought possible. Believe it firmly, expect it surely.

6

Preaching and Prayer

We are familiar with the vision of the valley of dry bones. We know that the Lord said to the prophet: "Prophesy upon these bones. . . . Behold, I will cause breath to enter into you, and ye shall live" (Ezek. 37:4, 5). When he had done this, there was a noise, and bone came together to its bone, and flesh came up, and skin covered them—but there was no breath in them. The prophesying to the bones—the preaching of the Word of God—had a powerful influence. It was the beginning of the great miracle which was about to happen, and there lay an entire army of men newly made. It was the beginning of the work of life in them, but there was no spirit there.

Then the Lord said to the prophet: "Prophesy unto the wind, . . . Thus saith the Lord God; Come from the four winds, O breath, and breathe upon these slain, that they may live" (v. 9). When the prophet had done this, the Spirit came upon them, and they lived, and stood on their feet, a very great army. Prophesying to the bones, that is preaching, has accomplished a great work. There lay the beautiful new bodies. But the prophesying to the Spirit, "Come, O Spirit," that is prayer, which has accomplished a far more wonderful thing. The power of the Spirit was revealed through prayer.

Is not the work of our ministers mostly this prophesying to dry bones in making known the promises of God? This is followed sometimes by great results. Everything which belongs to the form of godliness has been done to perfection; a careless congregation becomes regular and devout, but still it remains true for the most part that "there is no life in them." Preaching must be followed by prayer. The preacher must come to see that his preaching is comparatively powerless to bring in new life until he begins to take time for prayer and, according to the teaching of God's Word, he strives, labors and continues in prayer, and he takes no rest, and gives God no rest, until He bestows the Spirit in overflowing power.

Do you not feel that a change must come in our work? We must learn from Peter to continue in prayer, in our ministry of the Word. Just as we are zealous preachers, we must be zealous in prayer. We must, with all our power, constantly like Paul, pray unceasingly. For the prayer: "Come, breathe on these slain," the answer is sure.

7

Wholeheartedness

Experience teaches us that if anyone engages in a work in which he is not wholehearted, he seldom succeeds. Imagine a student or his teacher, a man of business, or a warrior. Any one of them who does not give himself wholeheartedly to his calling is not likely to succeed. That is still more true of spiritual work, and above all of the high and holy task of prayer to a holy God, and of being always well pleasing to Him. It is because of this that God emphasized: "Ye shall seek me, and find me, when ye shall search for me with all your heart" (Jer. 29:13).

Many of God's servants have said: "I seek Thee with my whole heart," but have you ever thought how many Christians there are of whom it is all too plain that they do not seek God with the whole heart? When in trouble over their sins, they seemed to seek God with the whole heart. But once they knew that they had been pardoned—even when one could see by their lives that they were religious—no one would think: "This man has surrendered himself with his whole heart to follow God, and to serve Him as the supreme work of his life."

How is it with you? What does your heart say? Even

though you have given yourself up with wholehearted devotion to fulfill your office faithfully and zealously (even as a minister, perhaps), maybe you need to acknowledge: "I fear—I am convinced—that the cause of my unsatisfactory prayer life is that I have not lived with a wholehearted surrender of all on earth that could hinder my fellowship with God." What a deeply important question to consider in our prayer closet and then give the answer to God! How important to arrive at a plain answer, and to confess it all before God! Prayerlessness cannot be overcome as an isolated thing. It is closely related to the state of the heart. True prayer depends on an undivided heart.

But I cannot give myself that undivided heart which can enable me to say: "I seek God with my whole heart." No, that is impossible for you, but God will do it. "I will give them a heart to fear me." "I will write my law [as a power of life] in their heart." Such promises serve to awaken desire. However weak the desire may be, if there is only a sincere determination to strive after what God holds out to us, then He himself will work in our hearts, both to will and to do. It is the great work of the Holy Spirit in us to make us willing. He enables us to seek God with the whole heart. May there but be found in us confusion of face because, while we have given ourselves to so many earthly things with all our heart and strength, if anything is said about fellowship with our glorious God, it so little affects us that we have not sought Him with our whole heart.

8

"Follow Me"

The Lord did not say these words to all who believed on Him, or who hoped to be blessed by Him, but only to those whom He would make fishers of men. He said this not only when He first called the Apostles, but also later on to Peter: "Henceforth thou shalt catch men." The holy art of winning souls, of loving and saving them, can be learned only in a close and persistent relationship with Christ. What a lesson for ministers and for Christian workers and others! This intimate relationship was the great and peculiar privilege of His disciples. The Lord chose them that they might be always with Him and stay near Him. We read of the choice of the twelve Apostles in Mark 3:14: "And he ordained twelve, that they should be *with him*, and that he might send them forth to preach." So also our Lord said on the last night (John 15:27): "And ye also shall bear witness, because ye have been *with me* from the beginning."

This fact was noticed by outsiders. Thus, for instance, the woman who spoke to Peter: "This man was also *with him*." So in the Sanhedrin: "They took knowledge of them, that they had been *with Jesus*."

The chief characteristic and indispensable qualification

for the man who will bear witness to Christ is that he has been with Him.

Continuous fellowship with Christ is the only school for the training of ministers of the Holy Spirit. What a lesson for all ministers! Only he who, like Caleb, follows the Lord fully will have power to teach other souls the art of following Jesus. But what an unspeakable grace, that the Lord Jesus himself wants to train us to be like Him, so that others may learn from us. Then we will be able to say with Paul to our converts: "Ye became followers of us and of the Lord." "Be ye followers of me, even as I also am of Christ."

Never has a teacher taken such trouble with his scholars as Jesus Christ will with us who preach His Word. He will spare no pains; no time will be too limited or too long for Him. In the love which took Him to the cross, He wants to fellowship and converse with us, fashion us, sanctify us, and make us fit for His holy service. Dare we still complain that it is too much for us to spend so much time in prayer? Shall we not commit ourselves entirely to the love which gave up all for us, and look upon it as our greatest happiness now to have fellowship with Him daily? Oh, all you who long for blessing in your ministry, He calls you to be *with Him.* Let this be the greatest joy of your life; it will be the surest preparation for blessing in your service.

O my Lord, draw me, help me, hold me fast. Day by day teach me how to live in Your fellowship by faith.

9

The Holy Trinity

1. God is an ever-flowing fountain of pure love and blessedness.

2. Christ is the reservoir wherein the fullness of God was made visible as grace, and has been opened for us.

3. The Holy Spirit is the stream of living water that flows from under the throne of God and of the Lamb.

4. The Redeemed, God's believing children, are the channels through which the love of the Father, the grace of Christ, and the powerful operation of the Spirit are brought to earth to be imparted to others.

5. What a clear picture we get here of the wonderful partnership in which God includes us as dispensers of the grace of God! Prayer, when we principally pray for ourselves, is only the beginning of the life of prayer. The glory of prayer is that we have power as intercessors to bring the grace of Christ, and the energizing power of the Spirit, upon those souls which are still in darkness.

6. The more closely the channel is connected with the reservoir, the more certainly will the water flow unhindered through it. The more we are occupied in prayer with the fullness of Christ and the Spirit who proceeds from Him,

and the more firmly we abide in fellowship with Him, the more surely will our lives be happy and strong. This, however, is still only a preparation for the reality. The more we yield ourselves to fellowship and converse with the Triune God, the sooner we receive the courage and ability to pray down blessing on souls, on ministers, and on the Church around us.

7. Are you truly a channel which is always open, so that water may flow through you to thirsty ones in a dry land? Have you offered yourself unreservedly to God, to become a bearer of the energizing operations of the Holy Spirit?

8. Is it not, perhaps, because you have thought only of yourself in prayer that you have experienced so little of the power of prayer? Do understand that the new prayer life into which you have entered in the Lord Jesus can be sustained and strengthened only by the intercession in which you labor for the souls around you, to bring them to know the Lord. Oh, meditate on this—God is an ever-flowing fountain of love and blessing, and I, His child, am a living channel through which every day the Spirit and life can be brought to the earth!

10

Life and Prayer

Our life has a great influence on our prayer; just as our prayer influences our life. Man's entire life is a continuous prayer—to nature or to the world—to provide for his wants and make him happy. This natural prayer and desire can be so strong in a man (who also prays to God) that the words of prayer which his mouth utters cannot be heard. At times God cannot hear the prayer of your lips, because the worldly desires of your heart cry out to Him much more strongly and loudly.

The life exercises a mighty influence over prayer. A worldly life, a self-seeking life, makes prayer powerless and an answer impossible. With many Christians there is conflict between the life and prayer, and the life holds the upper hand. But prayer can also exercise a mighty influence over the life. If I yield myself completely to God in prayer, then prayer can conquer the life of the flesh and sin. The entire life may be brought under the control of prayer. Prayer can change and renew the whole life, because prayer calls in and receives the Lord Jesus and the Holy Spirit to purify and sanctify the life.

Because of their defective spiritual life, many people

think that they must work themselves up in order to pray more. They do not understand that only in proportion as the spiritual life is strengthened can the prayer life increase. Prayer and life are inseparably connected.

What do you think? Which has the stronger influence over you, five- or ten-minute prayers, or the whole day spent on worldly desires? Do not be surprised if your prayers are not answered. The reason may easily be that your life and your prayer clash with each other; your heart concentrates more on living than on praying. Learn this great lesson: My prayer must rule my whole life. What I request from God in prayer is not decided in five or ten minutes. I must learn to say: "I have prayed with my whole heart." What I desire from God must really fill my heart the whole day; then the way opens for a certain answer.

How sacred and powerful prayer is when it takes possession of the heart and life! It keeps one constantly in fellowship with God. Then we can literally say, "I wait on You, Lord, all day long." Let us be careful to consider not only the length of time we spend with God in prayer, but the power with which our prayer takes possession of our whole life.

11

Perseverance in Prayer

"It is not reason," said Peter, "that we should leave the word of God, and serve tables" (Acts 6:2). For that work deacons were chosen. And this word of Peter serves for all time and for all who are set apart as ministers. "We will give ourselves continually to prayer, and to the ministry of the word." Dr. Alexander Whyte once said: "I think sometimes, when my salary is paid to me so faithfully and punctually: the deacons have performed faithfully their part of the agreement; have I been just as faithful in my part, in persevering in prayer and the ministry of the Word?" Another minister said: "How surprised people would be if I proposed to divide my time between these two equally—one half given to prayer, the other to the ministry of the Word."

In the case of Peter, notice what perseverance in prayer meant. He went up on the roof to pray. There, in prayer, he received heavenly instruction as to his work among the heathen. There, the message from Cornelius came to him. There, the Holy Spirit said to him: "Rise, and go with the three men who seek thee." From there he went to Caesarea, where the Spirit was so unexpectedly poured out on the heathen. All this is to teach us that it is through prayer God

103

will give the instruction of His Spirit to enable us to understand His will, to let us know with whom we are to speak
and to give us the assurance that His Spirit will make His
Word powerful through us.

Have you ever considered why you have a salary and a
parsonage, and so are freed from the need of holding a job?
The reason is so you can continue in prayer and the ministry of the Word. That will be your wisdom and your power.
That will be the secret of a blessed Gospel ministry.

No wonder there is complaint about the ineffective spiritual life in minister and congregation, while that which is of
prime importance, perseverance in prayer, does not hold its
rightful place—first place.

Peter was able to speak and act as he did because he was
filled with the Spirit. Let us not be satisfied with anything
less than hearty surrender to and undivided appropriation
of the Spirit, as Leader and Lord of our lives. Nothing less
will help us. Then, for the first time, we shall be able to say:
"God hath made us able ministers of His Spirit."

12

Carnal or Spiritual?

There is a great difference between those two states, which is but little understood or pondered. The Christian who walks in the Spirit, and has crucified the flesh, is spiritual (Gal. 5:24). The Christian who walks after the flesh, and wishes to please the flesh, is carnal (Rom. 13:14). The Galatians, who had begun in the Spirit, were ending in the flesh. Yet there were among them some spiritual members, who were able to restore the wandering with meekness.

What a difference between the carnal and the spiritual Christian (1 Cor. 3:1-3)! With the carnal Christian, there may be much religion and much zeal for God and for His service. But it is for the most part in human power. With the spiritual, on the other hand, there is a complete subjection to the leading of the Spirit, a deep sense of weakness and entire dependence on the work of Christ—it is a life of abiding fellowship with Christ, brought into being by the Spirit.

How important it is for me to find out and plainly to acknowledge before God whether I am spiritual or carnal! A minister may be very faithful in his orthodoxy, and be most zealous in his service, and yet be so, chiefly, in the power of human wisdom and zeal. And one of the signs of this is that there is little pleasure or perseverance in fellowship with Christ through prayer. Love of prayer is one of the marks of the Spirit.

What a change is necessary for a Christian who is chiefly carnal to become truly spiritual! At first he cannot understand what needs to change or how it can take place. The more the truth dawns upon him, the more he is convinced that it is impossible unless God does the work. Yet to believe truly that God will do it requires earnest prayer. Meditation and a quiet, solitary place are indispensable, along with the death of all confidence in ourselves. But along this road there ever comes the faith that God can, God is willing, God will do it. The soul which earnestly clings to the Lord Jesus will be led by the Spirit to this faith.

How will you be able to say to others: "I . . . could not speak unto you as unto spiritual, but as unto carnal, even as unto babes in Christ"? (1 Cor. 3:1). It is impossible unless you yourself have the experience of having passed from the one state to the other. But God will teach you. Persevere in prayer and faith.

13

George Müller

Just as God gave the Apostle Paul as an example in his prayer life for Christians of all time, so in recent times He has also given George Müller as proof to His church how literally and wonderfully He still always hears prayer. Not only did God give him over a million pounds sterling in his lifetime to support his orphanages, but Mr. Müller also stated that he believed the Lord had given him more than thirty thousand souls in answer to prayer. These were not only from among the orphans, but also many others for whom he had prayed faithfully every day (in some cases for fifty years), in the firm faith that they would be saved. When he was asked on what ground he so firmly believed this, his answer was: "There are five conditions which I always endeavor to fulfill. In observing these I have the assurance of answer to my prayer:

1. "I have not the least doubt because I am assured that it is the Lord's will to save them, for He willeth that all men should be saved, and come to the knowledge of the truth (1 Tim. 2:4). Also, we have the assurance 'that if we ask any thing according to his will, he heareth us' (1 John 5:14).

2. "I have never pleaded for their salvation in my own

name, but in the blessed name of my precious Lord Jesus, and on His merits alone (John 14:14).

3. "I always firmly believed in the willingness of God to hear my prayers (Mark 11:24).

4. "I am not conscious of having yielded to any sin, for 'if I regard iniquity in my heart, the Lord will not hear me' when I call (Ps. 66:18).

5. "I have persevered in believing prayer for more than fifty-two years for some, and shall continue till the answer comes: 'Shall not God avenge his own elect, which cry day and night unto him?' "

Take these thoughts to heart and pray according to these rules. Let prayer be not only the utterance of your desires, but a fellowship with God, until you know by faith that your prayer is heard. The way George Müller walked is the new and living way to the throne of grace, *which is open for us all.*

14

Hudson Taylor

When Hudson Taylor as a young man surrendered unreservedly to the Lord, he received a strong conviction that
God would send him to China. He had read of George
Müller, and how God had answered his prayers for his own
support and that of his orphans. Mr. Taylor began to ask
the Lord to teach him also to trust God like that. But he felt
that if he wanted to go to China with such faith, he must
first begin to live by faith in England. He asked the Lord to
enable him to do this. He worked as a doctor's assistant,
and asked God to help him not to ask for his salary, but to
leave it to God to move the heart of the doctor to pay him at
the right time. The doctor was a good-hearted man, but
very irregular in payment. This cost Taylor much trouble
and struggle in prayer because he believed like George
Müller, that the word, "Owe no man anything," was to be
taken literally, and that debt should not be incurred.

So he learned to move men through God—a profound
lesson, which later became an unspeakably great blessing to
him in his work in China. He believed that—in the conversion of the Chinese, in the awakening of Christians to give
money for the support of the work, in the finding of suitable

missionaries who would hold as faith's rule of conduct this—to make our desires known to God in prayer, and then to rely on God to move men to do what He would have done.

After some years in China, he prayed that God would give twenty-four missionaries, two for each of the eleven provinces and Mongolia, each with millions of souls and no missionary. God did it. But there was no society to send them out. He had indeed learned to trust God for his own support, but he dared not take upon himself the responsibility of the twenty-four. He feared they might not have sufficient faith. This cost him severe conflict and he became very ill under it, until at last he saw that God could just as easily care for the twenty-four as for himself. Then he assumed this responsibility in glad faith. And so God led him, through many severe trials of faith, to trust Him fully. These twenty-four increased, in course of time, to a thousand missionaries, who relied wholly on God for support. Other missionary societies have acknowledged how much they have learned from Hudson Taylor, as a man who stated and obeyed this law. "Faith may rely on God to move men to do what His children have asked of Him in prayer."

15

Light from the Inner Room

"But thou, when thou prayest, enter into thy closet, and when thou hast shut thy door, pray to the Father which is in secret; and thy Father which seeth in secret shall reward thee openly" (Matt. 6:6).

Our Lord spoke of the prayer of the hypocrites who desire to be seen of men, and also of the prayer of the heathen who trust in their many words. They do not understand that prayer has no value except when addressed to a personal God who sees and hears. In the text our Lord teaches a wonderful lesson concerning the inestimable blessing which the Christian may have in his secret place of prayer. To understand the lesson fully we must notice the light that the prayer room sheds on—

1. *The wonderful love of God.* Think of God, His greatness, His holiness, His unspeakable glory, and then imagine the inestimable privilege to which He invites His children, that each one of them, no matter how sinful or feeble, may have access to God anytime and may talk with Him as long as he wishes. God is ready to meet His child anytime he enters his prayer room, is ready to have fellowship with

him, to give him the joy and strength which he needs with the living assurance in his heart that God himself is with him and will undertake for him in everything. In addition, God promises that He will enrich His child in his outward life and work with those things which he has asked for in secret. Ought we not to cry out with joy? What an honor! What a salvation!

Do you see what an overflowing supply He offers for every need? One may be in the greatest distress, or may have fallen into the deepest sin. One may in the ordinary course of life desire temporal or spiritual blessing. Perhaps he wants to pray for himself or for those belonging to him, or for his congregation or church. He may even want to become an intercessor for the whole world—the promise for the prayer closet covers all: "Pray to thy Father which is in secret; He will reward thee openly."

We might well suppose that no place on earth would be so attractive to the child of God as the prayer room where the presence of God is promised and unhindered fellowship with the Father awaits. Think about the happiness of a child on earth who enjoys the love of his father, the happiness of a friend as he meets a beloved benefactor, or the happiness of a subject who has free access to his king and may stay with him as long as he wishes. All these joyful privileges are as nothing compared with this heavenly promise. In your prayer room you can converse with your God as long, as intimately as you desire. You can rely on His presence and fellowship there.

Do you see the wonderful love of God in the gift of a prayer room sanctified by such a promise? Let us thank God every day of our lives for it as the gift of His wonderful love. In this sinful world He could devise nothing more suitable for our needs, as a fountain of unspeakable blessing.

2. *The deep sinfulness of man.* Perhaps we think that every child of God takes advantage of such an invitiation with joy. But, what is the response? From all lands there

comes a cry that private, personal prayer is, as a general rule, neglected by those who call themselves believers. Many make no use of that privilege; they go to church, they confess Christ, but they know little of personal fellowship with God. Many pray little but in a spirit of haste, and more as a matter of custom or for the easing of conscience, so that they cannot testify to any joy or blessing from it. What is more sad, many who know something of prayer's blessedness confess that they know little about faithful, regular, and happy fellowship with the Father, all during the day, as something which is just as necessary as their daily bread.

What makes the prayer room so powerless? Is it not the deep sinfulness of man, and his fallen nature's aversion to God, which make the world with its fellowship more attractive than being alone with the heavenly Father?

Do Christians truly believe the Word of God, where that Word declares that "the flesh" which is in them, "is enmity against God"? Do they walk too much after "the flesh," so that the Spirit cannot strengthen them for prayer? Do Christians allow Satan to deprive them of the use of the weapon of prayer, so that they are powerless to overcome him? Our response only shows the deep sinfulness of man because no greater proof exists than this—we neglect our private prayer closet and so turn our backs on the unspeakable love which gave us that privilege.

Sadder still is that even ministers of Christ acknowledge that *they know they pray too little.* The Word tells them that their only power lies in prayer: through that only—but through that certainly—they can be clothed with power from on high for their work. But it seems as though the power of the world and the flesh has bewitched them. While they devote time to their work and manifest zeal in it, the most necessary thing of all is neglected, and there is no desire or strength for prayer to obtain the indispensable gift of the Holy Spirit to make their work fruitful. God give us grace to understand the deep sinfulness of our nature as we see the neglected prayer room.

3. *The glorious grace of Christ Jesus.* Is there no hope of change? Must it be always thus? Or is there a means of recovery? There is, thank God!

The man through whom God has made known to us the message of the inner room is no other than our Lord Jesus Christ, who saves us from our sins. He is able and willing to deliver us from this sin, and He will deliver. He has not undertaken to redeem us from all our other sins, and then left us to deal with the sin of prayerlessness in our own strength. No. In this also we may come to Him and cry out, "Lord, if You will You can make me clean." "Lord, I believe; help my unbelief."

How can you experience this deliverance? By the well-known way along which every sinner must come to Christ. Begin by acknowledging, by confessing before Him, in a childlike and simple manner, the sin of neglecting and desecrating the inner room. Bow before Him in deep shame and sorrow. Tell Him that your heart has deceived you by the thought that you, in your own strength, could pray as you ought. Tell Him that through the weakness of "the flesh," the power of the world, and self-confidence, you have been led astray and that you have no strength to do better. Do this with your whole heart. By your own resolution and effort you cannot put things right.

In your sin and weakness come into your prayer room, and begin to thank God, as you have never thanked Him, that the grace of the Lord Jesus will make it possible for you to converse with your Father, as a child ought to do. Once again hand over to the Lord Jesus all your sin and misery, as well as your whole life and will, for Him to cleanse and take possession of you, and rule over you as His very own.

Even though your heart may be cold and dead, persevere in the exercise of faith that Christ is an almighty and faithful Savior. You may be sure that deliverance will come.

Expect it. You will begin to understand that the prayer room is the revelation of the glorious grace of the Lord Jesus, which makes it possible for one to do what he could not do by himself—hold fellowship with God, and receive the desire and power which fit a man for walking with God.

PART THREE:

The Deepest Secret of Pentecost

1

The Cross-Spirit in Our Lord

Sometimes we seek for the operation of the Spirit, with the purpose of obtaining more power for work, more love in our life, more holiness in the heart, more light on Scripture or on our path. But all these gifts are only subordinate to what is the great purpose of God. The Father bestowed the Spirit on the Son, and the Son gave Him to us with the one great object of revealing and glorifying Christ Jesus himself in us.

The heavenly Christ must become for us a real living personality, always with us and in us. Our life on earth must be lived every day in unbroken and holy fellowship with our Lord Jesus in heaven. This must be the first and the greatest work of the Holy Spirit in believers, that they should know and experience Christ as the life of their life. God desires that we be strengthened with might by His Spirit in the inner man, so that Christ may dwell in our hearts through faith, and that in order to be filled with all the fullness of God's love.

This was the secret of the joy of the first disciples. They had received the Lord Jesus, whom they feared they had lost, as the heavenly Christ into their hearts. And this was their preparation for Pentecost: their attention was completely taken up with Him. He was literally their all. Their hearts were empty of everything, so that the Spirit might fill them with Christ. In the fullness of the Spirit they had power for a life and service such as the Lord desired. Is this the great object in our desires, in our prayers, in our experience? The Lord teaches us to know that the blessing for which we have so earnestly prayed can be preserved and increased in no other way than by faithfully cultivating intimate fellowship with Christ in our prayer room day by day.

But it has seemed to me that there was a still deeper secret of Pentecost to be discovered. The thought came that perhaps our conception of the Lord Jesus in heaven was too limited. We think of Him in the splendor and glory of God's throne. We also think of the unsearchable love which moved Him to give himself for us. But we forget too often that, above all, He was known here on earth as the Crucified One. Above all, it is as the Crucified One He has His place on the throne of God. "And, lo, in the midst of throne . . . stood a Lamb as it had been slain" (Rev. 5:6).

As the Crucified One He is the object of the Father's eternal good pleasure and of the worship of the entire creation. It is, therefore, of prime importance that we here on earth should know and have experience of Him as the Crucified One, so that we may make men see what His disposition and ours is, and also what the power is that can make them partakers of salvation.

I feel deeply that the cross is Christ's highest glory. The Holy Spirit neither has done nor can He do anything greater or more glorious than He did when He "through the eternal Spirit offered himself without spot to God" (Heb. 9:14). Because of that it is evident that the Holy Spirit can do nothing greater or more glorious for us than to take us up into the fellowship of that cross, and also work out in us the same spirit of the cross which was seen in our Lord Jesus.

The question arose: "Was this the real reason why our prayers for the powerful operation of the Holy Spirit could not be answered—had we sought too little to receive the Spirit who would help us to know and become like the glorified Christ in the fellowship of His cross?"

Is this the deepest secret of Pentecost? The Spirit comes to us from the cross, where He strengthened Christ to offer himself to God. He comes from the Father, who looked down with unspeakable good pleasure on the humiliation, obedience and self-sacrifice of Christ as the highest proof of His surrender to Him. He comes from Christ, who through the cross was prepared to receive from the Father the fullness of the Spirit, that He might share it with the world. He comes to reveal Christ to our hearts, as the Lamb slain, in the midst of the throne, so that we on earth may worship Him as they do in heaven. He comes especially to impart to us the life of the crucified Christ so that we may be able to say truthfully, "I am crucified with Christ. . . . I live, yet not I, but Christ liveth in me" (Gal. 2:20).

To understand this secret in any way, we must first meditate on the meaning and the value of the cross.

2

The Mind That Was in the Crucified Christ

The cross must necessarily be viewed from two standpoints. First, the work it has accomplished—the pardon and conquest of sin. This is the first message with which the cross comes to the sinner. It proclaims to him free and full deliverance from the power of sin. The second reveals the spirit or disposition which was there manifested. We find this expressed in Phil. 2:8: "He humbled himself, and became obedient unto death, even the death of the cross." Here we see self-abasement to the lowest place which could be found under the burden of our sin and curse; obedience to the uttermost to all the will of God; self-sacrifice to the death of the cross—these three words reveal to us the holy perfection of His person and work. Therefore God has greatly exalted Him. It was the spirit of the cross which made Him the object of His Father's good pleasure, of the worship of the angels, of the love and confidence of all the redeemed. The self-abasement of Christ, His obedience to the will of God even to death, His self-sacrifice even to the death on the cross—these made Him to be "the Lamb, as it had been slain, standing in the midst of the throne."

3

The Spirit of the Cross in Us

All that Christ was, He was for us and desires to become in us. The spirit of the cross was His blessedness and glory. It should be even more so for us. He desires to manifest His likeness in us, and to give us a full share of all that is His. Thus Paul writes the words we have so often quoted: "Let this mind be in you, which was also in Christ Jesus." Elsewhere he writes: "We have the mind of Christ." The fellowship of the cross is not only a holy duty for us, but an unspeakably blessed privilege, which the Holy Spirit himself will make ours according to the promise: "He shall take of mine, and shall show it unto you"; "He shall glorify me." The Holy Spirit formed this disposition in Christ and will also do it in us.

123

4

Taking Up the Cross

When the Lord told His disciples that they must take up the cross and follow Him, they could hardly have understood His meaning. He wished to rouse them to earnest thought, and so prepare them for the time when they should see Him carrying His cross. Onward from the Jordan where He had presented himself to be baptized and counted among sinners, He carried the cross always in His heart. That is to say, He was always conscious that the sentence of death, because of sin, rested on Him, and that He must bear it to the uttermost. As the disciples thought about this, and wondered what He meant by it, only one thing helped them understand—it was the thought of a man who was sentenced to death, and carries his cross to the appointed place.

Christ had said at the same time: "He that loseth his life shall find it." He taught them that they must hate their own life. Their nature was so sinful that nothing less than death could meet their need; it deserved nothing less than death. Gradually the conviction dawned on them that the taking up of the cross meant: "I am to feel that my life is under sentence of death, and that under the consciousness

of this sentence I must constantly surrender my flesh, my
sinful nature, to death." So they were slowly prepared to
see later on that the cross which Christ had carried was the
one power to deliver truly from sin, and that they must first
receive from Him the true spirit of the cross. They must
learn from Him what self-humiliation in their weakness and
unworthiness was to mean; what the obedience was which
crucified their own will in all things, in the greatest as well
as in the least; what the self-denial was which did not seek
to please the flesh or the world. "Take thy cross and follow
me"—that was the word with which Jesus prepared His
disciples for the great thought that His mind and disposition might become theirs, that His cross might in very deed
become their own.

5

Crucified with Christ

The lesson which the Lord wished His disciples to learn from His statement concerning the taking up of the cross and the losing of their life finds its expression in the words of Paul, after Christ had died on the cross, and had been exalted on high, and the Spirit had been poured out. Paul says: "I am crucified with Christ. . . . God forbid that I should glory, save in the cross of our Lord Jesus Christ, by whom the world is crucified unto me, and I unto the world" (Gal. 2:20; 6:14). He wanted every believer to live so as to prove that he was crucified with Christ. He wanted us to understand that the Christ who comes to dwell in our hearts is the crucified Christ, who will himself, through His life, impart to us the true mind of the cross. He tells us that "our old man is crucified with him," and that "they who are Christ's have crucified the flesh." When they received by faith the crucified Christ, they gave over the flesh to the death sentence which was executed to the full on Calvary. Paul says "we have been planted together in the likeness of his death" (Rom. 6:5), and that therefore we must reckon that we are dead to sin in Christ Jesus.

These words of the Holy Spirit, through Paul, teach us that we must abide constantly in the fellowship of the cross, in fellowship with the crucified and living Lord Jesus. It is the soul that lives ever under the cover and shelter and deliverance of the cross that alone can expect constantly to glory in Christ Jesus and in His abiding nearness.

6

The Fellowship of the Cross

There are many who place their hope for salvation in the redemption of the cross, who understand little about the fellowship of the cross. They rely on what the cross has purchased for them, on forgiveness of sin and peace with God, but they can often live for a long time without fellowship with the Lord himself. They do not know what it means to strive every day after heart communion with the crucified Lord as He is seen in heaven—"A Lamb in the midst of the throne." How good it would be if this vision might exercise its spiritual power upon us, that we might really experience every day that just as certainly as the Lamb is seen there on the throne, so may we have the power and experience of His presence here!

Is it possible? Without doubt it is. Why did that great miracle happen? Why was the Holy Spirit given from heaven if it were not to make the glorified Jesus—"the Lamb standing, as slain, in the midst of the throne"—present with us here in our earthly surroundings? Let us endeavor to make this more plain in our further meditations.

128

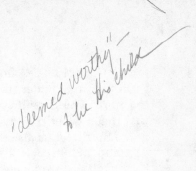
"deemed worthy" — to be His child

7

The Holy Spirit and the Cross

The Holy Spirit always leads us to the cross. It was so with Christ. The Spirit taught Him, and enabled Him to offer himself without spot to God.

It was so with the disciples. The Spirit, with whom they were filled, led them to preach Christ as the Crucified One. Later on He led them to glory in the fellowship of the cross when they were deemed worthy to suffer for Christ's sake.

And the cross directed them again to the Spirit. When Christ had borne the cross, He received the Spirit from the Father that He might be poured out. When the three thousand bowed before the Crucified One, they received the promise of the Holy Spirit. When the disciples rejoiced in their experience of the fellowship of the cross, they received the Holy Spirit afresh. The union between the Spirit and the cross is indissoluble; they belong inseparably to one another. We see this especially in the Epistles of Paul. "Jesus Christ hath been evidently set forth, crucified among you. . . . Received ye the Spirit by the works of the law, or by the hearing of faith?" (Gal. 3:1, 2).

"Christ hath redeemed us from the curse of the law . . . that we might receive the promise of the Spirit through faith" (Gal. 3:13, 14). "God sent forth his Son . . . to redeem them that were under the law . . . and . . . hath sent forth the Spirit of his Son into your hearts. . ." (Gal. 4:4-6). "And they that are Christ's have crucified the flesh. . . . If we live in the Spirit, let us also walk in the Spirit" (Gal. 5:24, 25). "Ye also are become dead to the law by the body of Christ . . . that we should serve in newness of spirit" (Rom. 7:4-6). "For the law of the Spirit of life in Christ Jesus hath made me free from the law of sin and death. For . . . God . . . condemned sin in the flesh: that the righteousness of the law might be fulfilled in us, who walk not after the flesh, but after the Spirit" (Rom. 8:2-4).

Always, in everything, the Spirit and the cross are inseparable—even in heaven. "In the midst of the throne . . . stood a Lamb as it had been slain, having . . . seven eyes, which are the seven Spirits of God sent forth into all the earth" (Rev. 5:6). Again: "He showed me a pure river of water of life, clear as crystal [Is this the Holy Spirit?], proceeding out of the throne of God and of the Lamb" (Rev. 22:1). When Moses smote the rock, the water streamed out and Israel drank. When the Rock Christ was actually smitten, and He had taken His place as the slain Lamb on the throne of God, there flowed out from under the throne the fullness of the Holy Spirit for the whole world.

How foolish it is to pray for the fullness of the Spirit if we have not first placed ourselves under the full power of the cross! Just think of the one hundred and twenty disciples. The crucifixion of Christ had touched, broken, and taken possession of their entire hearts. They could speak or think of nothing else, and when the Crucified One had shown them His hands and His feet, He said unto them: "Receive ye the Holy Ghost." And so also, with their hearts full of the crucified Christ, now received up into heaven, they were prepared to be filled with the Spirit. They dared to proclaim to the people: "Repent and believe in the Crucified One"; and they also received the Holy Spirit.

Christ yielded himself up completely to the cross. The disciples also did the same. The cross demands this also from us, it would have our entire life. To comply with this demand requires nothing less than a powerful act of the will, for which we are unfit, and a powerful act of God of which he may be assured who casts himself unreservedly, in helplessness, on God.

8

The Cross and the Flesh

These two are deadly enemies. The cross desires to condemn and put to death "the flesh." "The flesh" desires to cast aside and conquer the cross. Many, as they hear of the cross as the indispensable preparation for the fullness of the Holy Spirit, will find out what there is in them which must yet be crucified. We must understand that our entire nature is sentenced to death, and we must die, by the cross, so that the new life in Christ may come to rule in us. We must obtain such an insight into the fallen condition of our nature and its enmity against God, that we become not only willing but anxious to be wholly freed from it.

We must learn to say with Paul: "In me, that is in my flesh, dwelleth no good thing." "The mind of the flesh is enmity against God: it is not subject to the law of God, neither indeed can be." The very essence of "the flesh" is to hate God and His holy law. The wonder of redemption is that Christ has borne on the cross the judgment and curse of God on "the flesh," and has forever nailed it to the cursed tree. If a man only believes God's Word about this "cursed mind of the flesh," and then longs to be delivered from it, he learns to love the cross as his deliverer from the power of the enemy.

"Our old man is crucified" with Christ, and our one hope is to receive this by faith, and to hold it fast. "They that are Christ's have crucified the flesh." They have willingly declared that they will daily regard "the flesh" which is in them as the enemy of God, the enemy of Christ, the enemy of their soul's salvation, and will treat it as having received its deserved reward in being nailed to the cross.

This is one part of the eternal redemption which Christ has brought to us. It is not something which we can grasp with our understanding or accomplish through our own strength. It is something which the Lord Jesus himself will give us if we are willing to abide in His fellowship day by day, and to receive everything from Him. It is something which the Holy Spirit will teach us, and He will impart it to us as an experience, and will show how He can give victory in the power of the cross over all that is of the flesh.

9

The Cross and the World

What the flesh is in the small circle of my own person, so the world is in the larger circle of mankind. "The flesh" and "the world" are two manifestations of the same "god of this world" who is served by both. When the cross deals with "the flesh" as accursed, we at once discover what the nature and power of the world are: "They hated both me and my Father." The proof of this was that they crucified Christ. But Christ obtained the victory on the cross and freed us from the power of "the world." Now we can say: "God forbid that I should glory, save in the cross of our Lord Jesus Christ, by whom the world is crucified unto me, and I unto the world" (Gal. 6:14).

Every day the cross was to Paul a holy reality, both in what he had to suffer from the world and in the victory which the cross constantly gave. John also writes: "The whole world lieth in wickedness" (1 John 5:19). "Who is he that overcometh the world, but he that believeth that Jesus is the Son of God? This is he that came by water and blood, even Jesus Christ. . . . And it is the Spirit that beareth witness, because the Spirit is truth" (1 John 5:5, 6). Against the two great powers of the god of this world, God has given us two great powers from heaven, namely, the cross and the Spirit.

10

The Spirit and the Cross

Why are there not more men and women who can witness, with joyful hearts, that the Spirit of God has taken possession of them and given them new power to witness for Him? But another heart-searching question is more urgent: What is it that hinders? The Father in heaven is more willing than an earthly father to give bread to his child, and yet the cry arises: "Is the Spirit restricted or hampered? Is this His work?"

Many will acknowledge that the hindrance undoubtedly lies in the fact that the church is too much under the sway of the flesh and the world. They understand too little of the heart-piercing power of the cross of Christ. Because of that the Spirit does not have the vessels into which He can pour His fullness.

Many complain that the subject is too high or too deep for them. This is proof of how little we have appropriated and put into practice the teaching of Paul and Christ about the cross. I bring you a message of joy. The Spirit who is in you, in however limited a measure, is prepared to take you under His teaching, to lead you to the cross, and by His heavenly instruction to make you know something of what the crucified Christ wills to do for you and in you.

But then He wants you to take time, so that He may reveal the heavenly mysteries to you. He wants to make you see how the neglect of private prayer has hindered fellowship with Christ, the knowledge of the cross, and the powerful operations of the Spirit. He will teach you what is meant by the denial of self, the taking up of your cross, the losing of your life, and following Him.

In spite of all that you have felt of your ignorance, and lack of spiritual insight and fellowship with the cross, He is able and willing to teach you and make known to you the secret of the spiritual life above all your expectations.

Begin at the beginning. Be faithful in your prayer room. Thank Him that you can count on Him to meet you there. Even though everything may appear cold and dark, and you feel bound, bow in silence before the loving Lord Jesus, who so longs after you. Thank the Father that He has given you the Spirit. Be assured that all you do not yet know, and still need to learn—about "the flesh," and "the world," and the cross—the Spirit of Christ within you will surely make known to you. Only believe that this blessing is for you. Christ belongs entirely to you and He longs to obtain full possession of you. He can and will possess you through the Holy Spirit. But for this, time is necessary. Give Him time in prayer every day. You can rest assured that He will fulfill His promise in you. "He that loveth me keepeth my commandment, and my Father will love him, and I will manifest myself to him."

Persevere, in addition to all that you ask for yourself, in prayer for your congregation, your church, your minister; for all believers; for the whole Church of God, that God may strengthen them with power through His Spirit, so that Christ may dwell in their hearts by faith. What a blessed time it will be when the answer comes! Continue in prayer. The Spirit will reveal and glorify Christ and His love, Christ and His cross, "as the Lamb slain standing in the midst of the throne."

A Challenge

Our Head Christ took the lowest place on the cross, and so He has marked out for us His members, the lowest place. The brightness of God's glory (Heb. 1:3) became the rejected of men (Isa. 53:4). Since that time the only right we have is to be the last and the lowest. When we claim anything more we have not yet rightly understood the cross.

We seek for a higher life, and we shall find it if we sink deeper into the fellowship of the cross with our Lord. God has given the Crucified One the highest place (Rev. 5). Shall we not do the same? We do this when from hour to hour we act as those who are crucified with Him (Gal. 2:19, 20). In this way we honor the crucified Lord.

We long for full victory. We find this as we more fully enter into the fellowship of His cross. The Lamb obtained His greatest victory with His hands and feet nailed to the cross. We abide in the shadow of the Almighty only so long as we abide under the shadow of the cross. The cross must be our home. There alone are we sheltered. We first understand our own cross when we have understood His. And we desire to get so close to it that we not only view it but touch it; and still more that we take up the cross, and so it be-

138

comes an inner cross. Then the cross asserts itself in us, and we experience His power especially manifested in this, that we do not faint under it but carry it with joy.

What would Jesus be without His cross? His pierced feet have bruised the head of the enemy, and His pierced hands have despoiled him utterly (Matt. 12:29). What are we without the cross? Do not let the cross go, but hold it fast. Do we think that we can go by another road than that He trod? Many make no progress because they will not take up the cross.

Epilogue

A single word to the reader concerning the disposition of mind to which this book appeals! It is not enough that one should understand and appropriate the thought of the writer, and then rejoice because of the new insight he has obtained and the pleasure which knowledge has brought. There is something else which is of great importance. I must surrender myself to the truth, so that I shall be ready, with an undivided will, immediately to perform all that I shall learn to be God's will.

In a book such as this, dealing with the life of prayer and hidden fellowship with God, it is indispensable that we should be prepared to receive and obey all that we see to be according to the Word and will of God. Where this disposition to receive and obey is lacking, knowledge only serves to make the heart less capable of receiving fuller life. Satan endeavors to become master of the Christian's prayer time. Why? Satan knows that if one has been unfaithful in prayer, his testimony will bring but little loss to his kingdom. Spiritual power to lead the unsaved to the Lord, or to build up the children of God, will not flow from a prayerless life. This power comes only from persevering prayer.

The great living question is: Shall we earnestly set ourselves to win back again the weapon of believing prayer which Satan has, in a measure, taken away from us? Let us set before ourselves the serious importance of this conflict. As far as each minister is concerned, everything depends on whether or not he is a man of prayer—one who in the inner room must be clothed each day with power from on high. We, in common with the church throughout the whole world, have to complain that prayer has not the place in our service of God that it ought to have, according to the will and promise of God, and according to the need of minister and congregation and church.

The public consecration which many a believer has made at conferences is not an easy thing. And even when the step is taken, old habits and the power of the flesh will tend to nullify it. The power of faith is not yet vigorous. It will cost strife and sacrifice to conquer the devil in the name of Christ. Our churches are the battlefield where Satan will muster all his power to prevent us from becoming men of prayer, men who are powerful in the Lord to obtain victory in heaven and on earth. How much depends on this for ourselves, for our congregations, and for God's Kingdom!

With fear and trembling, and much prayer, I have written what I trust will help to encourage Christians in this conflict. With a feeling of deep unworthiness I venture to offer myself as a guide to the place of prayer, which is the way to holiness, and to fellowship with God.

I have asked the Lord that He would give this book a place in some prayer rooms, and that He may assist the reader, when he sees God's will, to immediately yield himself to do it. In war, everything depends on each soldier being obedient to the word of command, even though it costs him his life. In our strife with Satan we shall not conquer unless each one of us stands ready, even in the reading of this simple book, to say from the heart: "What God says I will do; if I see that anything is according to His will, I will immediately receive it and act upon it."

May there be in each one of us a spirit of surrender to immediate obedience to all we read here which has been in accord with the Word of God.

God grant that, in His great grace, this book may prove a bond of fellowship by which we may think of and help one another, and strengthen each other for the conflict in prayer by which the enemy may be overcome and the life of God may be gloriously revealed!

Weekend
Pammie

Want to inform
your husband
wife -tips
Kenneth

Sure to let your husband
best friend
Book
J. Smith
5th